Love
Vegetables

ANNA SHEPHERD

Love Vegetables

DELICIOUS RECIPES
FOR VIBRANT MEALS

**Photography by Liz and
Max Haarala Hamilton**

WHITE LION
PUBLISHING

CONTENTS

Introduction

This is a cookbook that puts vegetables at the heart of every recipe. I'm not an evangelical vegetarian or vegan, but I do love vegetables with a great passion and they form the backbone of my cooking and food philosophy. I recognise that in order to love cooking vegetables, you must also love eating them: otherwise, what's the point in moving beyond roast potatoes or boiled broccoli? My hope is that the recipes in this book will guide and encourage you to cook with vegetables every day. Not because you should, but because they are simply irresistible when coaxed into their most delectable forms, of which there are endless possibilities.

In these pages, you'll learn how to transform cabbages into a meltingly tender centrepiece, with a smoky citrus butter balming each layer and crevice. No longer just another vehicle for hummus, cucumbers are given lead billing on page 70, where they're grilled to a smoky complexity and balanced out with aromatic peaches and creamy homemade burrata. Every recipe has been developed and written with one mission in mind: does it make the vegetable delicious? I think so, and I hope you'll find lots of inspiration for what to cook when you have 20 minutes, or 90. Give this book to anyone who gets a veg box delivery, or dabbles in vegetable husbandry, and they'll have a library of possibilities at their fingertips to make the most of roots, shoots and savoury fruits every day of the year.

The vegetables in this book

At the risk of outraging the botanists out there, I'm categorising vegetables in this book as parts of plants that are prepared and eaten as savoury foods. Technically, aubergines, courgettes, cucumbers, tomatoes, peppers, squashes and even chillies are botanically considered fruits, but in culinary terms at least are treated like vegetables. I also have my favourites, and for that reason, as well as what I hope will have broad appeal, the vegetables in this book aren't exhaustive. If you have an opportunity to try bitter cardoons (try them layered through the parmigiana on page 157) or delicate salsify (add to the savoury crumble on page 117), then I encourage you to, but the ingredients in the chapters that follow can generally all be found on supermarket or greengrocers' shelves. Greengrocers do a wonderful job of selling vegetables when they're fresh and at their best – you're also more likely to find more unusual vegetables like romanesco cauliflowers and Jerusalem artichokes (sunchokes).

How to use this book

Whenever I start planning what to cook for dinner, I open the fridge drawer and investigate the vegetables. What am I craving? How much time do I have? My meals start with what ingredients I have that are fresh and nourishing (vegetables), and what follows are the other flavour and texture accessories that can show them off to their best advantage; a scatter of crunch or mood-enhancing burst of lemon can boost the confidence of even the shyest cabbage or cauliflower.

A quick scan will tell you that each chapter groups vegetables into categories (in Tender Greens, you'll find spinach, chard, beans and peas, for example). Loosely, these categories are vegetables which can bring a similar texture or vibe to a dish, and I'll highlight the qualities and similarities that make vegetables more adaptable than we give them credit for. Mineral spinach and earthy chard can play a similar role in a recipe; both work well with lemon, nutmeg, cream and anchovies, and I often swap one out for the other to save a shopping trip. Where there is an alternative vegetable that could be used to make the recipe, I've highlighted it in the *Variations* at the bottom of the page, so a spinach recipe could be made with chard or kale instead, and vice versa, if that's what you have in the fridge. This freer approach to using fresh ingredients has helped me to reduce the food that I waste, and led to many varied and delicious suppers – I'm sure it's also meant an incidental lower spend on the weekly shop, too.

A note on cooking and ingredients

A common complaint I hear about vegetables is that they don't have the same flavour impact as meat or fish. I suspect that this is down to the different ways in which these products are sold: vegetables are usually completely unprocessed and closer to their natural state, requiring more work from the cook to make them ready for consumption. Meat, however, is purchased butchered, portioned, cured and often even pre-flavoured with spice, ready to be eaten after a few minutes in a frying pan or under the grill. Sausages, steaks and drumsticks rarely resemble the animal that they come from. In short, meat is often a familiar shortcut to what we see as a 'proper' meal. There's certainly a stigma with vegetables that they won't be as satisfyingly savoury. With a few skills up your sleeve, vegetables can be made even more delicious than meat, and become the focal point in your meals for a more balanced plate.

Seasoning with salt at each stage as well as tasting as you cook is essential to making every forkful as delicious as it can be. I've given guidelines in each recipe about when to add salt (*always* when you start frying onions, please!), but taste is subjective, so my best advice would be to taste when it's safe, and often. Layering seasoning throughout the recipe will highlight every vegetable and aromatic, and will mean that you use less salt overall. If an end result is bland, it will need a fistful of salt on the surface to give it a flavour boost.

I use anchovies, fish sauce and Parmesan cheese (which contains animal rennet) in my cooking, so if you are (or are cooking for) a vegetarian, leave them out or use alternatives. All herbs are fresh, including bay leaves and curry leaves, unless otherwise specified. It's worth noting that fresh bay and curry leaves freeze well, and can be used frozen, as fresh (the dried leaves lose their potency so are best avoided). Lemons and other citrus fruits are unwaxed.

This is not a book that will preach to you about dietary dogma. I love pasta, cheese and bread and know that a mint chocolate chip ice cream on a scorching day is as good for my soul as a smoky barbequed leek, anointed with a nutty salsa. Life is definitely about balance, but my body and my mind know that it's vegetables that keep me together. The skills I've learned as a cook and recipe writer for vegetable growers have armed me with the knowledge to tease delectable flavour from the humblest swede or celeriac. My hope is that the recipes here will motivate you to make vegetables the main event at more mealtimes through sheer temptation. I encourage you to choose your own adventures in flavour with your own original adaptations, creating new and enticing vegetable masterpieces from familiar ingredients.

1

ALLIUMS

Onions, shallots, leeks and/or garlic will be the starting point of most savoury recipes. There are a host of other vegetables in the family, but as with any great dynasty, some are more popular and successful than others. I'm covering the core five in this chapter: onions (red and white); shallots; leeks; spring onions (scallions); and garlic.

Onions Softened, browned, caramelised or pickled, onions generally range from fiery at the raw end of the spectrum to deeper and sweeter the longer they're cooked. Each variety comes with its own flavour characteristics, but the most common are long-storing yellow or brown onions, with golden papery skin. Red onions have a spicier character than others, so they're particularly good for pickling and grilling (broiling).

Shallots These little bulbs tend to come in two shapes – round and oval. I've written the recipes in this book with round shallots, which are smaller, but if you have the larger ones (called banana or Echalion shallots), use one for every two the recipe calls for. Shallots can be used in the same manner as onions, but they have a slightly milder profile.

Leeks Sweet, buttery and modest, leeks are a wonderful vegetable and I don't just say that because I love Wales. They tend to be used in cooking in the same way as other alliums – as a base flavour for savoury dishes on which more confident ingredients can stand. Their creamy, silky texture when cooked and mild flavour makes them very successful in a host of iconic national dishes.

Spring Onions (Scallions) Like leeks, spring onions are composed of a tight bundle of leaves that grow towards the sun. They're actually young onions (not young leeks, in spite of appearances), harvested before the bulb has swollen to its familiar round shape. With a mild, grassy and sweet flavour, they can be eaten raw, sliced into salads, or cooked in a fraction of the time of their mature counterparts.

Garlic Even though I curse whenever I have to peel more than four cloves for a recipe, garlic is indispensable in my kitchen. The potency level depends on how you chop and prepare garlic: the smaller it's chopped/crushed/minced, the more allicin (a smelly, sulphurous compound) will be released, resulting in a more intense garlic flavour.

Garlic-Dressed Charred Green Bean Salad

Full disclosure: I set my smoke alarm off countless times while writing this recipe, so open a door or window, and use the extractor fan.

Garlic is a true shapeshifter here, adding oomph to the crispy tofu, a savoury accent to the rice and crispy golden slivers to the green beans. Allowing the beans to rest, covered in the garlic dressing, encourages them to soften and absorb all the zingy flavours as the smokiness mellows.

TIMINGS: 1 HOUR
SERVES 4

For the tofu
300g (10½oz) extra firm tofu, drained
75g (2½oz/¾ cup) cornflour
    (cornstarch)
1 tbsp black sesame seeds
3 tbsp vegetable oil
2 tbsp light soy sauce
1 tbsp runny honey
1 garlic clove, crushed
1 green chilli, deseeded and
    finely chopped

For the rice
200g (7oz) basmati rice
Neutral oil, for greasing
1 lime, unwaxed
2 lime leaves
1 tsp pink peppercorns
1 garlic clove, peeled
1 tsp salt
400ml (14fl oz/1¾ cups) weak,
    hot vegetable stock

For the salad
400g (14oz) runner beans, stalks
    trimmed
2 tbsp vegetable oil
8 garlic cloves, finely sliced
2 tbsp toasted sesame oil
1 tbsp fish sauce
150g (5½oz) cherry tomatoes,
    quartered
200g (7oz) mangetout (snow peas)
50g (1¾oz) toasted peanuts, roughly
    chopped
Leaves from a small bunch of mint
1 lime, cut into wedges

Preheat the oven to 200°C/400°F/Gas 6.

Break the tofu into rough walnut-sized pieces. Squeeze the tofu pieces to extract as much liquid as possible, then lay a sheet of kitchen paper on a plate and arrange the tofu in an even layer. Cover with another piece of kitchen paper and weigh it all down with a plate placed on top. Set aside while you prepare the rest.

Rinse the rice in a sieve until the water no longer runs cloudy, then tip into a lightly greased 20 x 20cm (8 x 8in) square oven-proof dish. Peel half the skin from the lime in strips and nestle these among the rice, along with the lime leaves, pink peppercorns, garlic and salt. Roughly stir everything with a spoon to distribute the aromatics among the rice grains. Pour over the hot vegetable stock, then cover the pan tightly with foil and slide into the oven to bake for 20 minutes.

Use a sharp, Y-shaped peeler to remove the tough, stringy seams from either side of the runner beans by pulling it down the length of each bean. Set the beans aside while you fry the garlic. You'll be using the same pan to fry the next few elements, so opt for your largest frying pan from the get-go. Heat the vegetable oil in the frying pan over a medium–low heat and when ripples are visible on the surface of the oil, add the garlic and turn the heat down to low. Fry, stirring frequently with a spatula, until all of the garlic slices are golden, about 5 minutes. Use a spatula to scrape all of the garlic and oil into a mixing bowl large enough to contain the beans and tomatoes. Add the sesame oil, fish sauce and tomatoes to this.

This is the smoky part. Thoroughly wipe the pan out with a piece of clean kitchen paper and return the dry pan to a high heat. In batches of two or three, depending on the size of your pan, arrange the runner beans first in an even layer and cook for 5 minutes on one side without turning, pushing down occasionally with tongs or a spatula to form blisters on the surface. Turn the beans over and cook in the same way for 5 minutes on the other side. Remove to a chopping board, roughly cut into 3cm (1¼in) pieces and toss through the garlic and tomato mixture before covering the bowl with a plate to trap the steam, which will help the beans continue to soften. This steaming stage is the difference between a tender and a squeaky bean, so don't leave the bowl uncovered for too long.

Cook the mangetout for a minute each side in the same pan, pressing down on each pod once or twice to blister them. Toss through the garlic dressing along with the runner beans and cover again with the plate. Set the bowl aside to continue to steam and soften while you cook the tofu.

By now the rice should be done. Remove it from the oven, lift away the foil and squeeze over the juice of the lime. Fluff the rice grains up with a fork.

In a medium mixing bowl, stir the cornflour and sesame seeds together, then toss the tofu through to coat. Heat the vegetable oil in the same pan over a medium heat for 45 seconds, then lift the tofu pieces out of the cornflour mixture into the hot oil, shaking off the excess over the bowl before you transfer the tofu to the pan. Fry for about 5 minutes, turning the tofu until crisp on all sides. While the tofu is frying, mix together the soy, honey, garlic and chilli. When the tofu is golden and crisp all over, remove the pan from the heat, then pour over the soy and honey mixture and stir to combine. It should bubble and cling to the tofu.

To construct the salad, toss the peanuts and mint through the bean mixture along with the crispy tofu. Serve the salad with lime wedges and the rice alongside.

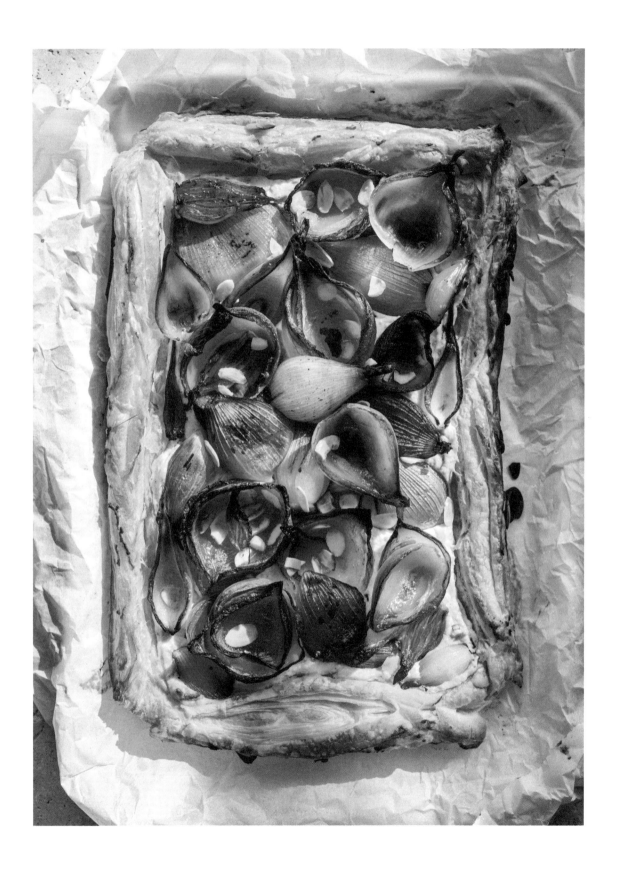

Red Onion Petal Pie

Cooking the onions in halves like this creates both a smoky note as they char in the pan, and a richly caramelised flavour as the sugars in the onions concentrate in the heat. This is one for you if you're a fan of French onion soup or caramelised onion tart.

TIMINGS: 45 MINUTES
SERVES 6

4 tbsp extra virgin olive oil
5 red onions, peeled and cut in half from top to bottom through the root
1 tbsp balsamic vinegar
1 tsp soft light brown sugar
1 x 320g (11¼oz) sheet ready-rolled puff pastry
1 egg, beaten
250g (9oz/1 cup) ricotta, drained
50g (1¾oz) feta, broken into small pieces
1½ tsp Dijon mustard
1 small bunch of chives, finely sliced
¼ whole nutmeg
1 tbsp flaked (sliced) almonds
½ small bunch of parsley
Salt and pepper

For the salad
1 small head radicchio
20 green grapes, roughly chopped
20g (⅔oz) toasted almonds, roughly chopped
½ small bunch of parsley, leaves and tender stems picked and roughly chopped
2 tbsp extra virgin olive oil
1 tbsp balsamic vinegar

Variations
Finely slice 4 leeks and caramelise them in a large frying pan before spreading over the cheese-topped pastry and baking for the same time.

Preheat the oven to 200°C/400°F/Gas 6.

Pour the oil into a medium-sized frying pan, ensuring the oil completely covers the base of the pan in a thin layer. Sprinkle in 1 teaspoon of salt and set over a medium heat. When the surface of the oil shimmers, lower in the onion halves, cut side down, so there's no overlap. Cover the pan with a lid and cook without peeking for 10 minutes. Meanwhile, mix together the balsamic vinegar and brown sugar.

Remove the onions from the heat and lay a sheet of baking parchment on a baking tray. Use tongs to place the onions, cut side up, on the tray. At this point, the flat side of the onions will look totally burnt, but this charring is what you want. Add a tablespoon of oil from the onion pan to the balsamic vinegar mixture. Brush the blackened surface of the onions with the vinegar mixture, then place in the oven for 20 minutes.

Meanwhile, line another baking sheet with baking parchment and unroll the pastry onto it. Use a sharp knife to score a 1cm (½in) thick border all around the edge. Prick the pastry inside the border all over with a fork. Brush the outside border with the beaten egg using the (cleaned) pastry brush. Tip the remaining egg into a mixing bowl and add the ricotta, feta, mustard and chives. Finely grate the nutmeg over the top and season generously with black pepper before stirring to combine everything together. Spread the ricotta mixture over the pastry, stopping at the egg-glazed border, then transfer to the fridge to chill.

Remove the onions from the oven and turn the temperature down to 180°C/350°F/Gas 4. Allow the onions to cool for a few minutes until you're able to handle them without burning yourself. Separate the layers, discarding the smallest inside layer, which will likely be totally carbonised.

Remove the pastry from the fridge and arrange the onion on top. Scatter over the flaked almonds. Place the tart in the oven to bake for 22–25 minutes, until the sides are puffed and golden.

While the pie is in the oven, separate the leaves of the radicchio, wash and dry. Toss with the other ingredients for the salad and season well.

Remove the pie from the oven and allow to cool for a few minutes before serving with the salad alongside.

Charred Spring Onions with Herby Breadcrumbs

Eggs and spring onions cook in roughly the same number of minutes (super quickly!), making this combo one of my go-to lunches when I'm working from home. It's my very crude spin on Turkish Çilbir (poached eggs on garlicky, spicy yoghurt), with a speedy flavour boost from rose harissa and smoky spring onions taking centre stage.

TIMINGS: 15 MINUTES
SERVES 2

2 eggs, at room temperature
2 bunches of spring onions (scallions)
200g (7oz/generous ¾ cup) full fat Greek yoghurt
2 tsp rose harissa
1 tsp baby capers in brine, drained and roughly chopped
1 x quantity Pangrattato (see page 181), replacing the parsley in the recipe with dill, plus a few sprigs to serve
2–4 slices of toast, to serve

Place a griddle pan on a high heat for at least 5 minutes to get it blazing hot before you start cooking.

Half fill a medium saucepan with water and bring to the boil. Lower in the eggs with a slotted spoon and set the timer for 6 minutes.

During this time, cook the spring onions on the griddle pan for 2–3 minutes, without moving them (this will help the char marks to form), before turning with tongs to mark the other side with black stripes for another 2–3 minutes.

Divide the yoghurt between two plates, then dollop half of the rose harissa on each portion. Ripple the rose harissa through the yoghurt with the back of a spoon. Arrange the spring onions on top of the yoghurt mixture and top with the capers and a spoonful of the herby breadcrumbs.

Remove the eggs from the water after 6 minutes. Pour the hot water from the saucepan and refill it with cold water from the tap. Lightly tap the eggs on a hard surface to crack the shell, then lower them into the cold water for a minute until they're cool enough to handle. Peel the eggs, starting from the wide end (where the air pocket is), then cut in half and place one on each plate over the spring onions. Scatter another spoonful of herby breadcrumbs over each halved egg. Pick a few sprigs of dill to garnish the spring onions and eggs and serve immediately, with slices of toast.

Any extra breadcrumbs can be stored in an airtight container for up to 5 days at room temperature and used to scatter over any of the pasta recipes in this book, instead of (or as well as) Parmesan.

Variations
Instead of spring onions, cook leeks according to the method on page 33, and serve with the other elements in the recipe.

My Favourite French Onion Soup

Years ago, I lived in Paris where twice a week I ate at *Le Sancerre* near Abbesses Métro with my two (eventually I'd make more) friends David and Bex. My order was always the *Soupe à l'Oignon Gratinée*, which, as well as being the cheapest thing on the menu, was also topped with a heart-attack-inducing molten mountain of cheese. This is a classic with a more reasonable amount of Comté.

TIMINGS: 1½ HOURS
SERVES 4

20g (⅔oz/1½ tbsp) unsalted butter
1 tbsp mild olive oil
1kg (2¼lb) brown onions, finely sliced
1 tsp soft light brown sugar
1 tbsp plain white (all-purpose) flour
2 garlic cloves, finely chopped
2 bay leaves
½ tsp dried rosemary
½ tsp dried thyme
½ tsp dried tarragon
1 tbsp Dijon mustard
1 tbsp white miso paste
200ml (7fl oz/generous ¾ cup) dry
   white wine
1.5 litres (52fl oz/6½ cups)
   vegetable stock
Salt and pepper

To serve
8 thin slices of baguette, or fresh
   white bread cut to a similar size
1 garlic clove, peeled
100g (3½oz) Comté cheese,
   finely grated
4 tbsp dry sherry, such as Fino or
   Manzanilla

Variations
There is no better version of this soup with other alliums. You could use up other strong, hard cheeses instead of Comté to top this soup, however, with Gruyère, hard goats' cheese and Cheddar all being successful alternatives.

Heat a large saucepan over a medium–high heat and add the butter and oil. When the butter is melted and bubbling noisily, tip the onions into the pan with a heaped teaspoon of salt. Stir for a couple of minutes to roughly break the onion layers up, then cover the pan with a lid and cook for 10 minutes, stirring occasionally, until the onions are completely soft. Remove the lid and turn the heat down to medium–low. Cook the onions, uncovered, for another 10 minutes, stirring every couple of minutes, until the onions are brown – by this point you might think they're caramelised, but time develops the sugars, so be patient.

Stir the sugar and a generous grind of black pepper through the onions, turn the heat down to low and continue to cook, uncovered, for another 25–30 minutes, until the onions are caramelised and have reduced in volume by three quarters.

Turn the heat back up to medium, sprinkle over the flour and cook for another couple of minutes, then stir through the garlic and fresh and dried herbs. After a minute, stir the mustard and miso through the onion mixture, then pour over the wine. Allow the wine to bubble away and reduce entirely (about 2 minutes), then pour over the vegetable stock. Bring to the boil, then turn the heat down to a simmer and cook, uncovered, for 20 minutes, until the soup has thickened slightly – you should be able to see the liquid level retreating down the inside of the saucepan. At this stage, the soup can be cooled, then frozen in an airtight container for up to three months, or stored in the fridge for up to 5 days.

Turn the grill (broiler) on to high. Toast the slices of baguette, then rub one side of each piece with the garlic clove. Arrange the slices, rubbed-side-up, on a roasting tray that will fit under the grill. Top the baguette slices with the grated cheese, then melt under the grill until bubbling. Meanwhile, divide the sherry between warm bowls.

Ladle the soup over the top of the sherry, then place a couple of cheesy croutons on top of each soup portion and serve straightaway.

Garlicky Cheese on Toast with Chilli-Spiked Broccoli

I'm not trying to make cheese on toast 'healthy' by stealthily slinging in a few broccoli spears, but I genuinely do think this is a more balanced cheese on toast, as the brassica's mineral freshness is a welcome contrast to the rich, molten cheese. For such a quick plate of comfort food, this is a really easy way to add in an extra portion of veg for the day, without spending loads of extra time chopping and peeling.

TIMINGS: 15 MINUTES
SERVES 2

150g (5½oz) tenderstem broccoli, tough/dry ends trimmed
2 slices crusty bread, such as sourdough
6 garlic cloves, peeled
100g (3½oz) extra mature Cheddar cheese, grated
2 tsp wholegrain mustard
2 tbsp extra virgin olive oil, plus extra for drizzling
½ small red chilli, sliced thinly into rounds
Juice of ½ lemon
Flaky salt

Place the broccoli in the basket of a steamer and suspend over a pan of boiling water for 4 minutes. Remove from the heat and pat dry with a clean tea towel.

Lightly toast the bread, bruise two of the garlic cloves and use to rub both sides of each slice of toast. Set these rubbed cloves aside to use later. Turn the grill (broiler) onto high. Grate two more of the garlic cloves into a medium mixing bowl, then stir through the cheese and mustard to combine.

Place the toast on a baking sheet lined with foil and divide the cheese mixture over the two slices. Arrange the broccoli in an even layer on the same baking sheet and drizzle with oil. Toss to coat the spears with oil evenly. Place the cheesy toasts and broccoli under the grill and grill for 3–4 minutes, until the cheese is melted and bubbling.

Slice the remaining four (two whole and two rubbed) garlic cloves finely. Heat the oil in a small saucepan over a high heat for 30 seconds. Add the garlic and chilli and allow to sizzle on the hob for 30 seconds before removing from the heat. Pour the chilli and garlic-spiked oil over the grilled broccoli, then squeeze over the lemon juice.

Divide the cheese on toast between warm plates, with some of the broccoli on the side. Season the broccoli with flaky salt just before serving.

Variations
Use purple sprouting or a head of broccoli instead, cut into bite-sized pieces. You could also serve sliced spring greens (see page 36), steamed, then stirred through the garlic and chilli oil.

Jammy Shallot & Walnut Orecchiette

Unapologetically savoury, comforting and intriguing in equal measure, this pasta is full of wonderful contrasts; fragrant rosemary and hot chilli, both dancing with salty anchovies, bright lemon and earthy walnuts to make every bite a delight. It's a corker to have in your back pocket when the fridge is bare.

TIMINGS: 45 MINUTES
SERVES 4

3 tbsp extra virgin olive oil
25g (1oz/2 tbsp) unsalted butter
12 round shallots, finely sliced
12 anchovy fillets in oil
2 tsp roughly chopped rosemary leaves
¼ tsp dried chilli flakes
4 garlic cloves, finely sliced
400g (14oz) orecchiette pasta
1 lemon, skin peeled and finely chopped
50g (1¾oz) walnuts, toasted
50g (1¾oz) sundried tomatoes in oil
Salt
1 x quantity Pangrattato (see page 181), to serve

Heat the oil and butter in a medium frying pan over a medium–high heat and when the butter is melted and bubbling, add the shallots and a pinch of salt. Cook, stirring regularly for 2 minutes, just to soften the shallots, then turn the heat down to medium–low and continue to cook until the shallots are completely tender and have begun to colour, about 8 minutes.

Use a fork to lift the anchovy fillets out of the jar, then add to the pan with the shallots. Use the back of a wooden spoon to press down on the anchovy fillets to break them up a bit. As they cook, they'll melt into the shallots. After a couple of minutes, once they've almost disappeared into the shallot mixture, add the rosemary, chilli and garlic to the pan. Stir for a minute until fragrant, then turn off the heat.

Fill a large saucepan with water, cover and bring to the boil over a high heat. When the water in the saucepan is boiling, salt it generously and tip in the orecchiette. Boil for a minute less than the packet instructions, until the pasta is al dente. Drain the pasta, placing a large heatproof jug under the colander to catch the starchy cooking water.

Pound the lemon peel, walnuts and tomatoes into a paste using a pestle and mortar, then add to the pan with the shallot mixture and return to the lowest heat to warm through.

Pour the drained pasta into the pan with the walnut mixture, along with 250ml (9fl oz/1 cup) of the pasta cooking water. Cook over a low heat, stirring constantly until the rich, umami sauce coats every piece of pasta. If the sauce is quickly absorbed and the orecchiette stay stuck together like little stacks of bowler hats, add another 50–100ml (1¾–3½fl oz/ ¼–scant ½ cup) of pasta cooking water and continue to stir.

Taste the sauce before serving. I like the slightly bitter edge of lemon peel contrasting with the deeply savoury anchovies and caramelised shallots, but if you prefer a bright lift, juice the lemon and pour over the pasta. Stir to combine, then taste again and adjust until you're happy with the seasoning.

Serve the pasta in warm bowls with the pangrattato in a bowl on the table for spooning over.

Variations

Use four brown onions instead of the shallots, but allow 8-10 minutes extra cooking time on the medium heat.

Pea & Potato Gnocchi with Crispy Fried Garlic Butter

The range and quality of *gnocchi di patate* available now is good news for all of us in the market for easy dinner wins. Look for fresh gnocchi in the chilled aisles, which has a lighter texture and fewer weird ingredients than the chewy, vacuum-packed dumplings found near the dried pasta shapes.

I say this serves two to four because I find the portion recommendations on fresh pasta packs to be ungenerous. In our house, this would serve two adults and one toddler.

TIMINGS: 20 MINUTES
SERVES 2–4

50g (1¾oz/3½ tbsp) butter
4 garlic cloves, finely sliced
2 tbsp extra virgin olive oil
500g (1lb 2oz) shop-bought potato
   gnocchi
2 shallots, finely sliced
50ml (1¾fl oz/3½ tbsp) dry sherry,
   such as Fino or Manzanilla
100ml (3½fl oz/scant ½ cup) hot
   vegetable stock
100g (3½oz/1 cup) frozen peas
Leaves from ½ small bunch of mint,
   picked
Juice of ½ lemon
Salt and pepper
Parmesan cheese, to serve

Melt half of the butter in a small frying pan over a low heat. Add the garlic and continue to cook, tilting the pan occasionally, until every garlic slice looks golden, but not brown. Use a slotted spatula to lift the garlic pieces onto a plate lined with kitchen paper. Reserve the butter.

Melt the remaining butter in a large frying pan, for which you have a lid, over a medium heat. Add the oil, then tip in the gnocchi, separating any pieces which have stuck together. Fry without moving the pan for 4 minutes to allow the gnocchi to take on some colour and crunch on one side, then shake the pan to move the gnocchi around so that the other side is exposed to the heat. Stir occasionally for another 4 minutes.

Add the shallots to the gnocchi pan and stir for a minute before adding the sherry. Allow the sherry to be absorbed before pouring in the stock and peas. Cover the pan with a lid and steam for 3 minutes. Remove the lid and stir in the mint, followed by the lemon juice. Season with salt and pepper to taste.

Return the crispy garlic to the reserved butter and gently warm through if the butter has started to solidify. Divide the gnocchi between warm bowls and drizzle a spoonful of the garlic butter over each portion, ensuring some of the crispy garlic is in each bowl. Finely grate a dusting of Parmesan over each bowl and serve immediately.

Variations
Use a red onion instead of the shallots, but allow 5 minutes extra cooking time.

Olive Oil Braised Leeks with Butter Beans & Sizzled Mint

Cooking the leeks slowly in oil and aromatics like this only intensifies their mellow sweetness, and turns their fibrous layers tender and almost creamy. This does take a little time, but once cooked, they can be covered and kept for up to 5 days in the fridge before finishing everything else off.

TIMINGS: 1½ HOURS
SERVES 4

4 slim leeks (about 750g/1lb 10oz in total), outer leaves removed and white and light green stalk cut into 2cm (¾in) rounds (save the dark green parts for stock)
1 red chilli, scored with a sharp knife
5 sprigs of tarragon
4 bay leaves
6 pink peppercorns
350ml (12fl oz/1½ cups) extra virgin olive oil
1 lemon
Salt and pepper
Crusty bread, such as baguette, to serve

For the beans
Leaves from ½ small bunch of mint (about 30 leaves), picked
2 garlic cloves, finely sliced
2 bay leaves
1 x 700g (1lb 9oz) jar of butter beans
1 lemon
75g (2½oz) fresh goats' cheese

Variations
If you can find them in season, Catalan calçots can be used instead of leeks, and cooked in the same way.

If the leeks are particularly grubby, place the rounds in a large bowl of cold water, with plenty of room to swill around. After half an hour any grit and grubs should fall to the base of the bowl.

Pat the leeks dry with a clean tea towel, then nestle the rounds tightly, cut side up, in a 25cm (10in) sauté pan. Pack the chilli, herbs and peppercorns around the leeks, then peel the lemon and tuck the peel among the leeks. Juice the lemon and pour over the leeks. Cover with the oil and 100ml (3½fl oz/scant ½ cup) water and sprinkle over 2 teaspoons of salt. Cut a piece of baking parchment that will fit tightly inside the pan to cover the leeks. Cover the pan with a lid if you have one, or tightly with kitchen foil. Cook over a low heat, checking after 10 minutes to see whether the oil is bubbling (if not, increase the heat until it does, then reduce the heat down to low). Continue to cook gently for 1–1¼ hours until the leeks are meltingly tender to the point of a sharp knife.

About 25 minutes before you want to serve, lay a piece of kitchen paper over a cooling rack. Heat a couple of tablespoons of the oil from the leeks in a medium sauté pan over a medium–high heat. When the oil forms ripples in the pan add the mint leaves, which will sizzle straightaway, and cook for about 90 seconds, stirring with a slotted spatula so the leaves don't clump together. When the leaves look translucent and brittle and the sizzle has died down completely, they're done. Lift onto the prepared rack with the slotted spatula while you cook the rest.

Pour a further 2 tablespoons of the leek oil into the same pan and set over a medium heat. Add the garlic and bay leaves, then pour in the beans and all of their liquid and squeeze in the lemon juice. Season well with pepper and taste to check for salt (jarred beans tend to be saltier than canned). Cook for 15 minutes before lifting the leeks out of their oil with a slotted spoon and stirring through the bean mixture. Cook the leeks and beans together gently for 10 minutes until the leeks are warmed through, then transfer to a platter and top with the mint and crumbled goats' cheese. Any extra oil can be kept stored in a jar in the fridge for up to a month and can be used to dress salads or whizzed into mayonnaise.

Serve the leeks with crusty bread.

Spiced Spring Onion Fritters with Garlic Yoghurt

These fritters make great party food, or a fun and zingy starter, and are fresh and light, unlike many other deep-fried things. Chopping the coriander stems adds extra brightness to the batter. Any tender herbs can be treated in the same way – usually the stems need cooking whereas the leaves can be used raw.

TIMINGS: 30 MINUTES
SERVES 4 (MAKES ABOUT
16 FRITTERS)

2 bunches of spring onions (scallions) (about 18–20)
Stems from ½ small bunch of coriander (cilantro)
1 green chilli, deseeded and finely chopped
1 tsp cumin seeds
1 tsp black mustard seeds
1 tsp ground turmeric
50g (1¾fl oz/⅓ cup) gram (chickpea) flour
Vegetable or sunflower oil, for frying
80ml (2¾fl oz/⅓ cup) cold lager
Salt and pepper
Lime wedges, to serve

For the salad
10 cherry tomatoes, quartered
½ cucumber, chopped into 1cm (½in) chunks
Juice of 1 lime
Leaves from ½ small bunch of coriander (cilantro)
1 small thumb ginger

For the garlic yoghurt
200g (7oz) natural yoghurt
1 garlic clove, grated

Variations

Replace 4 of the spring onions with a couple of shallots or 1 red onion for a bright pop of colour, taking care to separate the layers before adding to the batter.

Toss the tomatoes and cucumber for the salad together in a mixing bowl with a pinch of salt and the juice of half the lime and set aside.

Remove the roots and any dry or discoloured tops from the spring onions, then cut them into 6cm (2½in) lengths. Finely slice the lengths into thin strips, like those you might see on a Peking duck pancake. Drop the sliced spring onions into a medium mixing bowl. Finely slice the coriander stems and add them too (save the leaves for the salad), along with the green chilli. Toast the cumin and mustard seeds in a dry frying pan until you hear the mustard seeds start to pop, then tip into the bowl with the spring onions. Sift the gram flour and turmeric over the vegetables in the bowl, then toss to coat every piece of spring onion. Season well with salt and pepper.

Lay a couple of sheets of kitchen paper over a cooling rack and set it above a tray to the side of the hob. Pour the oil into a saucepan until it comes 6cm (2½in) up the sides, then clip a sugar thermometer to the side of the pan. When the oil reaches 170°C/340°F, pour the lager into the bowl with the vegetables and toss to form a batter, until no patches of flour are visible. If you don't have a sugar thermometer, drop a piece of white bread into the hot oil. It should turn golden and crisp in 30 seconds and bubble furiously as it does. Maintaining the temperature at 170°C/340°F, drop dessertspoons of the fritter mixture into the hot oil in batches of two or three, depending on pan size, and fry for 30 seconds before flipping the fritters over to cook for another 30 seconds on the other side. Using a slotted spoon, lift the cooked fritters out of the oil and drain on the kitchen paper while you repeat with the rest of the fritter mixture. Keep the cooked fritters warm in a low oven.

Add the coriander leaves to the bowl with the tomatoes and cucumber. Coarsely grate the ginger, then gather the grated ginger in your hand to squeeze the juice from the pulp over the bowl. Discard the grated ginger. Squeeze over the remaining lime juice and toss to combine. Adjust the seasoning to taste.

Mix the ingredients together for the garlic yoghurt in a bowl. Serve the fritters warm, alongside the salad, yoghurt and lime wedges.

Smoky Red Pepper Romesco & Grilled Leeks on Toast

My version of romesco contains a few shortcuts: jarred red peppers and tomato purée to speed things along. Perhaps not totally authentic, but this is something I make again and again, and I love to have it in the fridge to liven up almost anything. You'll make a little more than you need for this recipe. Any extra will keep covered in the fridge for up to 5 days.

TIMINGS: 30 MINUTES
SERVES 4

4 small leeks
Extra virgin olive oil, for drizzling
4 thick slices of crusty bread, such as sourdough
Salt

For the romesco
75g (2½oz) blanched almonds, toasted
2 large red (bell) peppers from the jar (about 120g/4¼oz), or cook your own (see page 120)
25g (1oz) stale bread, without crust, roughly torn
Leaves and tender stems from ½ small bunch of parsley
1 garlic clove
2 tsp sherry vinegar, plus extra if needed
100ml (3½fl oz/scant ½ cup) extra virgin olive oil
4 tbsp tomato purée (paste)
¼ tsp fennel seeds
1 tsp hot smoked paprika
Drizzle of honey, if needed
Salt and pepper

Variations
Instead of the leeks, blanch and grill whole asparagus spears.

Fill a large saucepan with water and bring to the boil.

While you're waiting for the water to boil, peel away the tough outer leaves from the leeks and cut away the darker green fibrous ends (save these for soup or stock). Just above the root, make a cut in each leek and draw the knife up the length of the leeks, keeping the root intact. With the roots pointing upwards, rinse the leeks under a running tap to dislodge any grit or dirt.

Once the water is at a rolling boil, add a big pinch of salt, then fully submerge the prepared leeks (if any are too long, trim them to size). Bring the water back to the boil, then set a timer for 3 minutes. Lay out a clean tea towel, and when the leeks have had their time, lift them out and onto the tea towel, spread out and leave to steam dry.

While they're drying, pulse together the first six ingredients for the romesco in a food processor to roughly chop. Pour the olive oil into a small saucepan and add the tomato purée. Cook over a medium–low heat, stirring regularly for 5 minutes, until the oil is stained red and the stop sign colour of the purée has deepened to a rusty tone. Remove from the heat and stir in the fennel seeds and paprika. The oil will remain separate from the purée, but everything will come together in the food processor. With the blade running, pour the oil mixture into the bowl of the food processor in a steady stream. Add salt and pepper to taste. Red peppers tend to be stored in a mixture of oil and vinegars of varying levels of acidity, so you may want to add a dash more vinegar, or a squeeze of honey to temper its sharpness.

Heat a griddle pan over a high heat until it's fiercely hot – this should take about 3 minutes. Grill the leeks, cut centres facing down and fanning out, for about 3 minutes on each side, leaving them without nudging too much to allow the striped black char marks to form. Remove from the griddle and drizzle with a little olive oil so they're glistening in places.

Toast the bread, then spread each slice with a generous heaped spoonful of romesco. Top with the grilled leeks and serve immediately. If you're particularly hungry, this combination is also delicious with a crispy fried egg (see page 48), or some grilled halloumi.

2

HARDY

GREENS

The vegetables in this chapter are probably my favourites to cook with because they're so interchangeable and have endless potential for adventures at dinnertime. Cabbages, kale, spring greens, broccoli, cauliflower and sprouts are all part of the same brassica family, and their similar bitter, mustardy characteristics make them easy to swap for one another with slight adjustments during the preparation stage.

Cabbagey Greens Versatile and delicious raw or cooked long and slow, tight and round brassicas including Brussels sprouts, majestic red cabbage and looser leafed white and green varieties are wonderful cooked in wedges until blackened in places, or shaved raw into slaws and salads for a fresh crunch with a vegetal heat.

Kales and Tougher Leafy Greens Spring greens are best when wilted either by steaming or blanching, or braised with olive oil or butter, whereas kale can do all that and turn into a vegetable crisp. Don't discard the tougher central light green stalk of either: simply chop and fry with shallots or garlic before stirring in the tender green leaves until softened and bright green. Collard greens (more common in the southern US states) can be cooked in a similar way to spring greens. Try them cooked down slowly, with plenty of garlic and a kick of chilli.

Broccoli, Cauliflower and Romanesco (Flowering Cruciferous Vegetables) Heads of cauliflower and broccoli can be roasted whole, or chopped into florets to be roasted with earthy spices like turmeric and cumin. The psychedelic romanesco has flower heads that grow into perfect fractals, unlike the little tree-like florets on cauliflower and broccoli heads. Long stem and sprouting varieties are much quicker to cook, but retain a deep savouriness that's enhanced by roasting or grilling.

Fresh Spiked Broccoli & Coconut Rice Larb Salad

I like to make this salad a bit more participatory and festive by laying out a few little gem leaves to use as cups to load the salad and coconut rice into so it can be eaten with hands. This is totally optional, and it's up to you whether you want to eat your salad in a bowl or in a lettuce cup, but the self-assembly nature of the latter is a lot of fun and has the added bonus of slowing everyone down while they eat.

<u>TIMINGS: 1 HOUR</u>
<u>SERVES 4</u>

For the rice
300g (10½oz/scant 1½ cups) Japanese short grain rice, plus 2 tbsp
1 x 400ml (14oz) can coconut milk
½ tsp caster (superfine) sugar

For the larb salad
300g (10½oz) extra-firm tofu
2 carrots, peeled and grated on the largest holes of a box grater
1 shallot, sliced into thin 1mm (⅟₃₂in) rounds
1 tbsp cornflour (cornstarch)
Neutral oil, such as peanut or sunflower, for shallow frying
1 tbsp light soy sauce
1 head broccoli (about 300g/10½oz), grated or very finely sliced on a mandoline
Bunch of spring onions (scallions), white and light green parts finely sliced at an angle into 2mm (⅟₁₆in) rounds
1 red chilli, finely sliced
1 green chilli, finely sliced
Leaves from a small bunch of mint, picked (larger leaves roughly torn)
Leaves from a small bunch of coriander (cilantro)
Fine sea salt

For the dressing
3 tbsp fish sauce
90ml (3fl oz/6 tbsp) freshly squeezed lime juice (roughly 3–4 limes)
1 tbsp soft light brown sugar
1 garlic clove, finely grated

To serve
2 heads little gem (baby bibb) lettuce, leaves separated (optional)
50g (1¾oz) toasted cashews or peanuts

Rinse the rice in a sieve, agitating the grains with your hands until the water underneath looks clear. Tip the rice into a mixing bowl and cover with 2cm (¾in) cold water. Set aside.

Lay a sheet of kitchen paper on a board. Break the block of tofu up into small crumbly pieces on the absorbent paper. You're aiming for the larger pieces to be roughly the size of a button mushroom. Cover the tofu with more kitchen paper and place another board on top to extract as much liquid as possible. This will result in crispy tofu, which is all the more receptive to the fresh dressing.

Toast the extra 2 tablespoons of rice in a frying pan without any oil. Keep the heat on medium–low and shake the pan regularly to toast the rice all over and prevent it from catching and burning in places. After about 8 minutes, the rice should be done when it's a rich golden colour all over and smells like popcorn. Tip it into a mortar and grind with a pestle until finely ground.

Drain the soaked rice, then tip into a saucepan. Pour in the coconut milk and add the sugar and ½ teaspoon salt. Cover the pan with a lid and bring the liquid to the boil. Turn the heat down to a simmer and continue to cook for 12 minutes. Remove the pan from the heat and leave the lid on while the rice steams for 10 minutes. After this time, remove the lid and fluff the rice with a wooden spoon. Cover with a lid again to keep the rice warm while you cook the rest.

While the rice is resting, mix all of the ingredients for the dressing together in a small mixing bowl. Toss the carrots and shallot together in a wide salad bowl and pour over one quarter of the dressing. Toss to combine, then gather the carrot mixture to one side of the bowl while you prepare the rest.

Heat enough oil to cover the base of a large non-stick frying pan over a medium–high heat. Toss the crumbly pressed tofu pieces with the cornflour in a small mixing bowl and season with a pinch of salt. Test the oil heat by dropping in a tofu piece; if it's hot enough to fry, it should sizzle and bubble straightaway. If it doesn't, continue to heat the oil before frying the tofu. Once frying, stir regularly until the pieces are crisp and golden all over. Lift out of the pan with a slotted spatula and place in the salad bowl with the carrots. Drizzle the tablespoon of soy sauce over the tofu and toss to combine, then nestle next to the carrots without mixing the two together.

Next, stir fry the broccoli. There should be a little oil left in the pan from the tofu, but if not add a small amount and heat over a medium–high heat. Add the broccoli to the pan, along with a pinch of salt and stir fry until the broccoli is tender, smoky and beginning to char in places. Tip the broccoli into the bowl with the tofu and carrots and add the spring onions, chillies, herbs and toasted rice. Set aside until you're ready to serve.

If you're serving the salad with the little gem and rice, get them ready on the table, along with the toasted nuts.

Drizzle the remaining dressing over the salad just before serving and toss to combine. Serve the salad with the rice on its own, sprinkled with toasted nuts, or loaded into little gem cups after a spoonful of the rice.

Variations
Replace the broccoli with cauliflower and cook in the same way.

Smoky Buttered Romanesco with Creamy White Beans

I worked for an organic veg box company in my twenties, teaching new skills with swede, and cooking vegetarian pop-up feasts around the country. Whenever I was 'on tour', I'd serve this hero dish with romanesco whenever it was in season. Without fail, we were always asked for this recipe when the dishes were cleared.

TIMINGS: 1¼ HOURS
SERVES 4

1 large romanesco (about 750g/1lb 10oz)
1 tbsp extra virgin olive oil, plus extra for drizzling
50g (1¾oz/3½ tbsp) unsalted butter
2 garlic cloves, finely sliced
1 red chilli, finely sliced
1 tsp hot smoked paprika
Leaves and tender stems of a small bunch of parsley
50g (1¾oz) almonds, toasted and roughly chopped
Salt and pepper

For the red onion pickle
1 red onion, very finely sliced into rounds on a mandoline
1 tbsp red wine vinegar
1 tsp caster (superfine) sugar

For the beans
2 tbsp extra virgin olive oil
2 garlic cloves, finely chopped
1 bay leaf
1 x 600g (1lb 5oz) jar butter beans, drained
200ml (7fl oz/generous ¾ cup) vegetable stock

Variations
Swap the romanesco for broccoli prepared and roasted for the same time (don't remove the foil during roasting as broccoli is prone to burning before it's cooked through).

Preheat the oven to 200°C/400°F/Gas 6.

Trim the base of the romanesco, discard any discoloured or very large, tough leaves, and set the remaining leaves aside. Cut a deep 'x' in the stalk of the romanesco, then place it snugly in a small, deep roasting dish and pour 100ml (3½fl oz/scant ½ cup) of water around the base. Cover the dish tightly with foil, then place in the oven for 30 minutes.

While the romanesco is steaming in the oven, make the red onion pickle. Scrunch the red onion in a small mixing bowl with the vinegar, sugar and a pinch of salt until the slices soften. Place a bowl or jar on top of the onions to weigh them down, then set aside.

Heat the olive oil for the beans in a small saucepan over a medium heat and add the garlic and bay leaf. Stir for 30 seconds until fragrant. Add the beans and stock to the pan. Cook, stirring occasionally, for 15 minutes.

Remove the foil from the romanesco and drizzle it generously with olive oil (there may be some water in the base of the dish, but this will continue to evaporate). Scatter over a little salt and pepper, then return it to the oven to roast for a final 15 minutes, until the romanesco is black in places, and tender to the point of a sharp knife. Seven minutes before the end of the cooking time, drizzle the reserved leaves with oil and arrange them around the whole vegetable.

To make the smoky butter, heat the oil and butter in a small frying pan over a low heat. When the butter is melted, stir in the garlic and chilli and continue to cook over a low heat for 7–8 minutes, until the garlic is golden. Remove from the heat and stir in the hot smoked paprika.

Lift the bay leaf out of the beans and use a stick blender to purée the mixture until smooth. Season generously with freshly ground black pepper.

Spread the bean purée over a large serving platter. Cut the romanesco into quarters and arrange on top of the beans. Finely chop three-quarters of the parsley and stir into the smoky butter, and pour it over the top of the romanesco. Scatter over the almonds and remaining parsley leaves. Drain the onion pickle and serve alongside.

Sweetheart Red Curry

This mildly spicy and creamy coconut curry is as rewarding to make as it is delicious to eat; whizzing up your own curry paste feels like kitchen alchemy (albeit simple blender magic). The smoky charred cabbage is a great, tender partner to the confidence of chilli, citrus and coriander. The curry paste makes double what you'll need for the curry, but any extra can be chilled (5 days) or frozen (6 months).

TIMINGS: 1 HOUR, PLUS SOAKING TIME
SERVES 4

For the curry paste
4 dried pointed chillies
3 shallots, halved
4 garlic cloves
1 red chilli, deseeded
1 green chilli, deseeded
2 stalks lemongrass, roughly chopped
1 x 6cm (2½in) piece galangal, peeled
1 x 6cm (2½in) piece ginger, peeled
Stalks from a small bunch of coriander (cilantro)
1 tsp fish sauce
4 lime leaves
½ tsp fine salt
50ml (1¾oz/3½ tbsp) vegetable oil

1 tbsp honey
1 tbsp tomato purée (paste)
1 tbsp ground cumin
2 tsp ground coriander
1 x 400g (14oz) can coconut milk
800ml (28fl oz/3½ cups) vegetable stock
1 tbsp fish sauce
200g (7oz) carrots, peeled, then peeled into long ribbons

To serve
Cooked rice
1 lime, cut into wedges
Leaves from a small bunch of coriander (cilantro)

For the curry
200g (7oz) firm tofu
2 tbsp vegetable oil
1 sweetheart or pointed cabbage, cut into quarters
1 tbsp soy sauce

Variations
Roast or grill (broil) halved Brussels sprouts, or cauliflower florets until tender and charred, then stir into the curry sauce.

Cover the dried chillies with boiling water and leave to soak for 20 minutes. Drain the chillies and add them to the bowl of a food processor with the other ingredients for the curry paste. Blitz until a smooth paste forms, scraping down the sides with a spatula a few times. You should have roughly 200g (7oz) curry paste from this mixture. Measure out 100g (3½oz) for today's curry.

Slice the tofu in half, then place it in between two pieces of kitchen paper and place a plate on top to weigh it down and extract as much liquid as possible.

Heat 1 tablespoon of the oil in a large, deep frying pan over a high heat. Fry the cabbage wedges cut-side down for 4 minutes until charred. Nudge the wedges over onto the other cut side and continue to fry, without moving around too much for another 3 minutes. This can be a smoky job. Lift the charred cabbage wedges onto a plate and set aside.

Cut the tofu into 2cm (¾in) cubes. Heat the remaining oil in the same pan and turn the heat down to medium. Fry the tofu cubes, turning every couple of minutes, until golden all over. Stir in the soy sauce and honey. Everything should bubble and turn syrupy almost immediately. Scrape the tofu and its sauce onto a separate plate and wipe the pan out.

Return the pan to a medium heat and add the curry paste. Fry for 3 minutes until fragrant, then add the tomato purée and continue to fry for 5 minutes, stirring regularly to prevent the paste from sticking – if it does, add a splash of water. Stir in the dried spices and continue to cook for a minute until fragrant, then pour in the coconut milk, vegetable stock and fish sauce and stir to combine. Add the carrots and stir again. Arrange the cabbage quarters around the pan, so that there's no overlap, but the cabbage isn't submerged by the sauce. Sprinkle a teaspoon of salt over the vegetables and sauce, then bring the curry sauce to the boil. Turn the heat down to a simmer and cook, uncovered, for 25 minutes until the curry sauce has thickened, adding the tofu 5 minutes before the end of the cooking time.

Spoon the curry into warm bowls and serve with rice, lime wedges and a scattering of coriander leaves.

Orecchiette with Shaved Brussels Sprouts & Brown Butter Hazelnuts

The idea for this dish was inspired by an interview I read with chef Margot Henderson describing the cabbage pasta with truffle oil that her now husband Fergus cooked for her when they were first dating. She said she thought to herself: 'God, he's cool' (cabbages are cool!). Brussels sprouts are really like little cabbages, so being in miniature makes them cute *and* cool.

TIMINGS: 20 MINUTES
SERVES 2

For the pasta
400g (14oz) Brussels sprouts
200g (7oz) dried orecchiette
1 tbsp extra virgin olive oil
20g (⅔oz/1½ tbsp) unsalted butter
2 shallots, finely chopped
1 green chilli, finely chopped (seeds and all)
2 garlic cloves, finely chopped
Salt and pepper
Parmesan cheese, to serve

For the brown butter hazelnuts
30g (1oz/2 tbsp) unsalted butter
50g (1¾oz) hazelnuts, toasted and roughly chopped
1 sprig rosemary, leaves picked and chopped

Variations
Very finely slice 400g (14oz) of Savoy cabbage, discarding the core and root. Fry the cabbage for 4 minutes before stirring in the shallots, chilli and garlic.

Fill and boil the kettle.

Cut the root end off the Brussels sprouts and place the flat cut sides of the sprouts down on the chopping board. Finely slice each sprout into thin pieces, turning it on its side when your knife gets perilously close to your fingertips to chop it into even pieces. Alternatively, use a mandoline to shave the sprouts finely – use a finger guard if you do! Keep the prepared sprouts in a bowl until ready to use.

Tip 1 litre (35fl oz/1¼ cups) of the boiling kettle water into a saucepan and add a tablespoon of salt. Bring to the boil again, add the orecchiette and boil for 1 minute less than the packet instructions.

While the pasta boils, heat the butter for the hazelnuts in a small saucepan over a medium heat. When the butter has completely melted it will turn foamy on top, then these solids will fall to the base of the pan under the surface of the melted butter which will turn a rich brown and smell toasty. At this stage, remove from the heat (it will take about 5 minutes in total). Stir in the hazelnuts and rosemary and set aside.

For the sprouts, heat the olive oil and butter together in a deep frying pan over a medium heat. When the butter is melted and sizzling, tip in the shallots, chilli and garlic and fry for a couple of minutes until the shallots have softened and everything in the pan is fragrant. Add the sprouts and season generously with salt and pepper. Turn the heat up to high and cook, stirring regularly until the sprouts are deep brown in places and tender. Taste to check that they have lost most of their bitterness.

Drain the pasta, reserving 150ml (5fl oz/scant ⅔ cup) of the cooking water. Tip the pasta into the pan with the sprouts, along with the cooking water and turn the heat down to medium. Stir continuously until the starchy pasta cooking water coats every piece of orecchiette to form a creamy sauce.

Spoon the pasta into warm bowls, then spoon half of the brown butter over each portion. Top with finely shaved Parmesan and an extra crack of black pepper.

Pantry Greens & Beans Soup

I make a version of this soup when I'm feeling thinly spread: it's very low effort/high reward and extremely nourishing without tasting worthy. Be generous when drizzling the olive oil over the soup; it's a wonderful carrier of flavour and elevates the greens from grassy to unctuous.

TIMINGS: 50 MINUTES
SERVES 4

2 leeks
4 tbsp extra virgin olive oil, plus extra
    for drizzling
1 carrot, peeled and finely chopped
1 stick celery, finely chopped
Bunch of parsley
2 bay leaves
4 garlic cloves
1 cinnamon stick
1 x 400g (14oz) can borlotti beans,
    drained
1.2 litres (40fl oz/5 cups) low-salt
    vegetable or chicken stock, or
    bouillon
200g (7oz) cavolo nero, roughly
    chopped
Salt and pepper

For the soup topping
1 garlic clove
1 lemon
25g (1oz) very finely grated Parmesan
    cheese
1 tsp cornflour (cornstarch)
Neutral oil, for frying
Flaky salt

Very finely chop the white end of the leeks, discarding the root. Set these lighter parts aside. Where the leaves turn green and begin to fan out, finely slice a handful and set aside.

Heat the olive oil in a large saucepan over a medium–high heat and add the white leek slices, along with the carrot and celery. Sprinkle over 2 teaspoons of salt and a big grind of black pepper and cook, stirring occasionally, for 15 minutes until the leeks are sweet and translucent and the vegetables have reduced in volume by half. Meanwhile, separate the parsley stalks and leaves and finely chop the stalks. Add the parsley stalks to the saucepan after the vegetables have had their 15 minutes. Turn the heat down to medium. Very finely chop the parsley leaves and tip them into a small mixing bowl. Set aside for the soup topping.

After 5 minutes, stir in the bay leaves, garlic and cinnamon and cook for a couple of minutes until fragrant. Add the beans, vegetable stock and cavolo nero to the pan and bring to the boil. Turn the heat down to a simmer and cook, covered with a lid, for 15 minutes, until the cavolo nero is wilted.

For the soup topping, very finely chop the garlic and add to the bowl with the parsley. Zest over the lemon, then stir in the cheese. Cut the lemon in half and squeeze the juice into the soup.

Toss the reserved leek slices in the cornflour, then pour 2mm (1⁄16in) of oil into a small saucepan. Heat the pan over a medium–high heat. Lay a piece of kitchen paper over a cooling rack by the hob. Fry the leek slices for 2 minutes, stirring regularly. When the leeks are crispy and beginning to turn golden, lift out of the hot oil with a slotted spoon and transfer to the kitchen paper. Sprinkle immediately with flaky salt.

Before serving, taste the soup and adjust the seasoning. Ladle into warm bowls and serve with a teaspoonful of the topping and a handful of crispy fried leeks. Drizzle a generous pour of extra virgin olive oil over the top.

The soup can be made up to 5 days in advance and kept covered in the fridge (without the crispy leeks on top). It usually benefits from having time to allow the flavours to mingle and tastes better the day after it's made.

Variations
Use other hardy greens, such as finely sliced Savoy cabbage, ribbons of spring greens or curly kale.

Cashew & Cauliflower Rice with Chimichurri

Appearing relentlessly on menus everywhere over the past few years, this brassica is the champion social climber. The spices in the rice and chimichurri are inspired by the sunshine flavours of South America. Instead of the crispy egg, try serving the rice alongside a curry (see Sweetheart Red Curry on page 43).

TIMINGS: 30–40 MINUTES
SERVES 4

For the chimichurri
2 bay leaves
100ml (3½fl oz/scant ½ cup) extra virgin olive oil
½ large bunch of parsley, leaves picked
3 sprigs oregano, leaves picked
3 garlic cloves
1 red chilli
Pinch of dried chilli flakes
2 tbsp red wine vinegar
Salt

For the cauliflower rice
1 large cauliflower (about 1kg/2lb 2oz)
3 tbsp neutral oil, for frying
1 celery stick, halved lengthways, then roughly chopped
2 shallots, roughly chopped
1 green chilli, deseeded and finely chopped
1 heaped tsp cumin seeds
1 cinnamon stick
100g (3½oz) frozen peas
75g (2½oz) cashews, toasted and roughly chopped

To serve
Neutral oil, for frying
4 eggs
Dried chilli flakes
Flaky salt
1 lime, cut into wedges

Place the bay leaves in a small saucepan, along with the extra virgin olive oil. Heat gently on the hob until the bay leaves begin to crackle, then remove from the heat and leave to infuse while you prepare the rest.

Finely chop the parsley, oregano, garlic cloves and red chilli and add them to a small bowl with the chilli flakes and ¼ teaspoon salt. Set aside.

Peel any discoloured or tough leaves away from the cauliflower, then roughly chop the cauliflower into large florets and tender leaves. Roughly peel and chop the tough central stalk. Pulse everything in the food processor until the cauliflower is broken down into small pieces resembling couscous. If you don't have a food processor, use a box grater to grate the whole cauliflower for a similar result.

Heat the oil in a large frying pan over a medium heat, then add the celery and shallots along with a pinch of salt and fry for 4–5 minutes, until the vegetables soften. Stir in the chilli and spices and fry for a minute until fragrant. Next, tip in the cauliflower and turn the heat up to high. Sprinkle over half a teaspoon of salt and fry, stirring regularly for 8–10 minutes, until the cauliflower has lost a quarter of its volume and is charred in places. Push the cauliflower to one side of the pan and tip in the peas. Leave the peas to steam for a minute before stirring into the cauliflower, along with the cashews.

Divide the cauliflower rice between warm bowls and keep warm in a low oven heated to 150°C/300°F/Gas 2 while you cook the eggs.

Heat enough oil to cover the base of a large frying pan. Turn the heat up to high. Crack four eggs into the pan, spacing them out, to allow for crispy edges. Sprinkle each of the egg whites with a modest pinch of chilli flakes. Fry the eggs for a couple of minutes, tilting the pan and spooning the hot oil over the whites to ensure they cook through. Cook the eggs until the whites are set, but the yolks are runny. Use a spatula to place an egg on top of the rice in each bowl.

Remove the bay leaves from the olive oil and pour over the parsley and chilli mixture. Stir in the red wine vinegar. Taste and adjust the seasoning if needed. Spoon a little chimichurri over the egg whites with some flaky salt and serve with lime wedges.

Variations
Broccoli can be blitzed and cooked into 'rice' in the same way - you might need two heads. Peel the broccoli stalk before blitzing.

Holiday Broccoli

This smoky broccoli is inspired by a dish I ate at The Pot Luck Club in Cape Town. I think the broccoli must have been cooked over a wood fire, and it was the best thing I'd eaten all holiday. Marinating the broccoli in yoghurt tenderises it before cooking, and tempers its bitter sulfurous character, too. I serve rice noodles alongside to make a complete meal.

TIMINGS: 45 MINUTES
SERVES 4

For the broccoli
100g (3½oz/scant ½ cup) Greek yoghurt
1 garlic clove
1 tsp curry powder
500g (1lb 2oz) broccoli
Salt

For the spicy peanut sauce
2 banana shallots, roughly chopped
1 red chilli, deseeded and roughly chopped
1 green chilli, deseeded and roughly chopped
4cm (1½in) piece of ginger, peeled and roughly chopped
2 garlic cloves
6 lime leaves
2 tbsp coconut oil
2 tsp medium curry powder
1 tbsp soy sauce
5 tbsp smooth peanut butter
2 tsp fish sauce
2 tsp honey
Juice of 1 lime

For the noodles
200g (7oz) rice noodles
1 tbsp toasted sesame oil
2 tsp soy sauce
1 tsp black sesame seeds

To serve
Toasted peanuts, roughly chopped
Coriander (cilantro) leaves
1 lime, cut into wedges

Mix the yoghurt, garlic and curry powder together in a large mixing bowl, then season with 1 teaspoon of salt. Cut the broccoli into generous bite-sized florets. Peel the stalk, then cut it into rough 2cm (¾in) cubes. Transfer the broccoli to the bowl with the yoghurt mixture and toss to combine. The broccoli can be marinated up to 6 hours in advance, or at least while you get on with the rest.

Blitz the shallots, chillies, ginger, garlic and lime leaves together with a pinch of salt in a food processor until a paste forms. Melt the coconut oil in a small saucepan over a medium–low heat and scrape the chilli and shallot mixture into the pan. Cook, stirring regularly, for 5 minutes, until the mixture seems to firm up, having lost some of its liquid, and is intensely fragrant. Remove from the heat and stir in the remaining ingredients, adding 100ml (3½oz/scant ½ cup) of warm water to loosen the mixture. Taste and adjust the seasoning.

Preheat the grill (broiler) to high.

Spread the broccoli out on a large roasting tray in an even layer. Cook under the grill for 10–12 minutes, removing the tray every couple of minutes to turn the broccoli so that it cooks evenly. Remove from the grill when the broccoli is tender and charred in places.

Cook the noodles according to packet instructions. Drain, and while still warm transfer to a mixing bowl and toss in the sesame oil, soy sauce and sesame seeds to coat.

To serve, divide the noodles between warm bowls and top with broccoli. Drizzle a couple of tablespoons of sauce over the top and sprinkle with toasted peanuts and coriander. Serve with lime wedges for squeezing over.

You'll end up with more peanut sauce than you need, and although I could eat it by the spoonful, it's better deployed to liven up dishes down the line (it will keep covered in the fridge for up to a month). Try it drizzled over grilled chicken, tossed through a rice salad with fresh herbs and spring onions (scallions), or alongside steamed greens.

Variations
Use tenderstem or purple sprouting broccoli instead. Cut the stalks and florets into bite-sized pieces before marinating.

Chilli Butter & Citrus Savoy Cabbage

I suggest the crinkled Savoy or January King cabbages for this recipe because their leaves are thick and structured, allowing the sharp and spicy chilli butter to cling to the crevices and caramelise between the layers.

TIMINGS: 1¼ HOURS
SERVES 6

For the cabbage
2 Savoy or January King cabbages (about 1.2kg/2lb 11oz)
2 onions, quartered
250ml (9fl oz/1 cup) boiling water
12g (⅓oz/2½ tsp) salt
150g (5½oz/⅔ cup) unsalted butter, melted
75ml (2½fl oz/5 tbsp) extra virgin olive oil
1 orange
1 lime
2 lemons
6 garlic cloves, crushed
4 tbsp rose harissa
2 tbsp tomato purée (paste)
1 tsp Turkish chilli flakes (pul biber)
½ tsp dried chilli flakes
1 tsp hot sauce (such as Tabasco)
3 mixed pointed chillies (red and green), roughly chopped
1 tbsp honey

For the polenta
1.2 litres (40fl oz/5 cups) hot vegetable stock
300g (10½oz) quick cook polenta
30g (1oz/2 tbsp) unsalted butter
1 tbsp rosemary leaves, roughly chopped
100g (3½oz) crumbly Cheshire or Lancashire cheese, grated

Preheat the oven to 220°C/425°F/Gas 7.

Cut each cabbage into six wedges through the root, which should hold each wedge together. Arrange the cabbages in one large, or two roasting trays so that they're in an even layer with no overlap. Nestle the onions among the cabbages. In a jug, stir together the boiling water and the salt until the salt dissolves. Pour the salty brine over the vegetables, then cover the tray(s) tightly with kitchen foil and transfer to the oven.

While the cabbage is cooking in the oven, mix the butter and olive oil together with the juice of the orange, lime, one of the lemons and the remaining ingredients for the cabbages. Stir with a fork to combine.

Remove the vegetables from the oven after 20 minutes and lift away the foil. Pour over the citrus–chilli butter mixture to coat every wedge. Return the vegetables to the oven and roast for a further 35–45 minutes, removing the tray(s) three or four times to baste the buttery mixture over the vegetables. Remove the wedges from the oven when they're meltingly tender, and the outer leaves and craggy edges are charred.

Ten minutes before the vegetables are finished, pour the stock for the polenta into a large saucepan. Bring to the boil, then pour the polenta into the boiling liquid in a steady stream, stirring constantly. Still stirring, bring the mixture to the boil, then turn the heat down to a simmer to cook according to packet instructions, stirring regularly (in my experience this ranges from 1–8 minutes). Beat in the butter, rosemary and cheese, then remove from the heat.

Spoon the polenta into warm bowls and top with a couple of wedges of cabbage and a generous drizzle of the chilli butter mixture from the roasting pan. Cut the remaining lemon into wedges for squeezing over the cabbage and polenta. Any extra cabbage wedges can be chopped and stirred through cooked pasta with ricotta or cream.

Variations
Cook cauliflower or romanesco in the same manner as the cabbages, and serve alongside the chilli butter and polenta.

3

TENDER

GREENS

Some people panic when they don't have milk or butter in the fridge, but I'm anxious if I don't have a bag or bundle of quick-cooking greens or tender vegetables that can be stir fried, grilled or sautéed in minutes to make dinner more vibrant.

Tender and delicate leafy vegetables really get me animated these days, because they're often the most exciting thing to eat on the table. Sure, they require some preparation (no one likes gritty or watery greens) and a touch of magic with complementary flavours like chilli, garlic and lemon, but once you've mastered a few techniques, there's a whole world of thrilling dishes that will make you want to weave a portion of greens into every meal.

Leafy Spinach, chard, Chinese leafy green vegetables such as pak choi and Chinese broccoli, and peppery leaves are wonderful just frightened into tenderness by a flash in the steamer or pan. Once cooked, they're best squeezed or steamed dry, making them all the more receptive to other ingredients. If you're adding them to something saucy (such as a curry or stew), roughly chop and stir in while raw, so that the leaves absorb the spices and aromatics.

Peas, Green Beans, Mangetout I suspect these vegetables are offered to children as a slightly sweeter alternative to more serious greens like broccoli and cabbage. My experience was that they were usually steamed or boiled and just served as is. Great if they're just picked and of the best quality, but if they've been in plastic for 5 days in the fridge, they'll certainly need a bright lift from fresh herbs and a splash of vinegar or citrus. Try charring in a pan (see page 13) or dressing while hot with ginger, garlic, chilli and lime.

Long Tender Greens I know that someone will tell me that courgettes (zucchini) are, in botanical terms, not a vegetable but a berry, but treated like vegetables and charred, braised or grated into little fritters, they are one of my absolute favourites — and versatile, too. Cucumbers (from the same family) are usually chopped into salads or pickled, but they can be a revelation when cooked (see page 70). Other options abound, but notably asparagus, which is a treat and super quick to cook. Try it instead of toast soldiers with a soft-boiled egg.

Mac & Cheesy Greens Filo Pie

A pasta pie might seem indulgent (bonkers, even?) on paper, but as a Big Fan of Stanley Tucci, this is my homage to the timpano in his film *Big Night*. The *Big Night* pie consists of layers of pasta, meatballs, eggs, salami, tomato sauce and more pasta, but this one is a great deal lighter.

Verdant macaroni and cheese is encased in a delicate filo pastry shell, making this an easy but beautiful crowd-pleaser. Serve with a dressed salad, chopped tomatoes, or roasted root vegetables on the side.

TIMINGS: 1 HOUR,
PLUS RESTING TIME
SERVES 6

750ml (26fl oz/3¼ cups) whole milk
2 bay leaves
2 garlic cloves
75g (2½oz/5 tbsp) unsalted butter, melted, plus 50g (1¾oz/3½ tbsp)
8 sheets of filo (phyllo) pastry
250g (9oz) spinach, chard or spring greens
Leaves from a large bunch of parsley
Leaves from a large bunch of basil
400g (14oz) macaroni
50g (1¾oz) plain white (all-purpose) flour
100g (3½oz) Cheddar cheese, grated
125g (4½oz) ball of Mozzarella cheese, torn
50g (1¾oz) Parmesan cheese, grated
1 tbsp Dijon mustard
¼ whole nutmeg
½ tsp black onion (nigella) seeds
Salt and pepper

Preheat the oven to 180°C/350°F/Gas 4.

Pour the milk into a saucepan and add the bay leaves and garlic cloves. Heat the milk over a medium heat until bubbles appear around the sides of the pan, but watch carefully, ensuring the milk doesn't come to the boil. Remove the pan from the heat, crack in a generous amount of black pepper, pour into a jug and cover. Set aside to infuse while you get on with the rest.

Brush the base and sides of a 23cm (9in) round springform tin with melted butter, then line the base with baking parchment. Lay a sheet of filo pastry over the tin, then tuck any overhanging filo into the tin, so that the pastry completely covers the base and comes up the sides, and brush all over with melted butter. Repeat with another five sheets of filo pastry (you'll want six layers in total), brushing each layer with melted butter, then cover the remaining two sheets of filo pastry with a clean tea towel on a clean kitchen surface, to prevent them from cracking and drying out.

Place the filo pastry-lined tin in the oven to partially bake for 5 minutes.

Rinse the spinach (or other greens) in a colander, then transfer to a large saucepan and cover with a lid. Wilt over a medium–low heat, using tongs to turn the leaves occasionally. When the greens are deep green and have reduced significantly in volume, transfer to a colander and allow to steam dry. Fill the pan with water (there's no need to wash it up), and place on the hob to boil.

Squeeze the greens dry and transfer to the bowl of a food processor with the parsley and basil, then lift out the garlic cloves from the milk and add them to the greens. Pulse to finely chop, then set aside. Alternatively, very finely chop by hand in two or three batches.

When the water in the saucepan has come to the boil, tip the pasta in along with a tablespoon of salt. Cook for 2 minutes less than the packet instructions, then drain in a colander.

While the pasta is on the boil, make the cheesy sauce. Melt the remaining 50g (1¾oz) butter in a large saucepan over a medium–low heat. Add the flour and stir for a couple of minutes to cook out the rawness from the flour. Then, stirring all the time, slowly pour in the infused milk and continue to cook for about 8 minutes, stirring often, until the sauce has thickened enough to coat the back of a wooden spoon. Remove from the heat and stir in the cheeses and mustard, and finely grate in the nutmeg. Remove the bay leaves, then add the greens and herbs to the sauce. Taste and add more salt and pepper if you like.

Decant the pasta into the cheesy green sauce, then stir well to coat every piece of pasta. Spoon the saucy pasta into the partially baked pastry case, then drape a sheet of filo over the top and brush the surface with melted butter. Arrange the final filo sheet in an attractive ruffle and brush again with more melted butter. Sprinkle over the black onion seeds and place the pie on the middle shelf in the oven.

Bake the pie for 30 minutes, checking after 20 minutes in case your oven has a hot spot, and the pie would benefit from a turn to cook the pastry evenly. Remove the pie from the oven and allow to cool in the tin for 20 minutes. This will ensure the slices don't collapse as soon as you cut into it, but it will still be meltingly hot.

Release the pie from the springform tin and transfer to a serving plate. Use a serrated knife to cut the pie into six slices.

Variations
Use the same quantity of curly kale or cavolo nero (remove the tough white ribs before steaming), instead of the leafy greens.

Lemony Garlic Greens with Chickpeas

This has all the zip and thrill of a bracing bowlful from South East Asia (think citrussy aromatics and pointed little chillies), but with flavours more firmly rooted in Italy.

Scale it up with another can of chickpeas and more fresh veg, but be sure to increase the liquid quantities so the bright sauce glazes every chickpea. I often serve this with some crispy fried feta alongside (see page 121).

TIMINGS: 40 MINUTES
SERVES 2

75ml (2½fl oz/5 tbsp) extra virgin olive oil, plus extra for drizzling
2 onions, finely sliced
1 lemon
2 sticks of celery, finely sliced
6 garlic cloves, finely sliced
2 green chillies, finely chopped
½ tsp dried chilli flakes
1 x 600g (1lb 5oz) jar chickpeas, drained
250g (9oz) chard, tough stalks finely sliced and leaves roughly torn
150ml (5fl oz/scant ⅔ cup) vegetable stock
100ml (3½fl oz/scant ½ cup) white wine
10 cherry tomatoes, finely chopped
Splash of red wine vinegar (optional)
Leaves from a small bunch of parsley
Salt and pepper
Crusty bread, to serve

Heat the olive oil in a large, deep sauté pan over a medium heat for 1 minute. Add the onions, a pinch of salt and generous grind of black pepper and stir to combine. Cook for 8 minutes, stirring the onions occasionally, until they're tender and just beginning to colour. While the onions are cooking, peel and finely chop the skin of the lemon, setting the fleshy part aside. Add the lemon skin to the onions along with the celery and cook for another 4 minutes, stirring to make sure nothing catches and burns. Add the garlic and both chillies and stir for a minute more until fragrant.

Pour the chickpeas into the pan with the chard stalks and cook for a couple of minutes until the stalks are no longer tough (taste one to check). Add the leaves, stock and white wine and allow the sauce in the pan to thicken at a gentle simmer for 10–15 minutes.

Meanwhile, taste some of the cherry tomatoes and if they don't sing, toss in a bowl with a splash (no more than ¼ teaspoon) of red wine vinegar and pinch of salt and set aside while the chickpeas and greens cook. Any shy-flavoured, out of season tomatoes can be treated this way to bring them out of their shell. Roughly chop the parsley.

Stir the parsley into the chickpeas and remove from the heat. Cut the peeled lemon in half and use your hands to squeeze over the juice. Spoon the chopped tomatoes over the top and drizzle all over with extra olive oil. Spoon the chickpeas, greens and some of their sauce into warm bowls and serve with crusty bread for mopping up the sauce that your spoon can't catch.

Variations
Replace half the weight of chard with mangetout (snow peas) or string beans.

Tomato Braised Green Beans with Garlic & Bay

Cooking beans for this long will feel counter-intuitive, but it's mostly hands-off and their slow-braised texture is really special. They turn silky soft and take on loads of flavour from the tomatoes, so every bite tastes like sunshine. I look for stringless runner beans to save the job of peeling the fibrous strands from each side, but this can just as easily be made with a combination of string beans along with the runner beans, or with string beans alone.

TIMINGS: 2 HOURS
SERVES 4

5 tbsp extra virgin olive oil
2 large onions, finely sliced
8 garlic cloves, finely sliced
4 bay leaves
2 tbsp tomato purée (paste)
1 x 400g (14oz) can peeled plum tomatoes
750g (1lb 10oz) stringless runner beans, stalks removed
Leaves from a small bunch of basil
2 tsp red wine vinegar
Salt and pepper
Crusty bread and cheese, or cooked pasta, to serve

Heat 2 tablespoons of the oil in a large, deep saucepan, for which you have a lid, over a medium–high heat. Add the onions to the pan, along with ½ teaspoon of salt. Cook, stirring occasionally, for 10–12 minutes, until the onions are softened and beginning to take on some colour. Add the garlic and bay leaves to the pan and continue to cook for a minute until the garlic and bay are intensely fragrant. Stir in the tomato purée and cook for 5–7 minutes, until the colour of the purée changes from traffic light to rust red.

Add the tomatoes from the can, along with a pinch of salt. Half fill the can with water and swill the can with the water to loosen the tomato liquid from the sides of the can. Pour the water into the pan and cook for 3–4 minutes. In the meantime, cut the beans into 3cm (1¼in) angled pieces. Stir the beans and the remaining oil into the tomato mixture and turn the heat down to low. Cook for an hour and a half with the lid on, stirring occasionally.

After this time, taste the beans. They should be meltingly tender. Stir in the basil and continue to cook for 5 minutes. Season with the red wine vinegar, salt and pepper.

Serve the beans on their own, with crusty bread and cheese, or stirred through cooked pasta.

The beans can be made up to 5 days in advance and kept covered in the fridge. Bring them up to room temperature, or warm through gently before serving.

Variations
Replace the beans with fennel, sliced into 1cm (½in) pieces, cooked for the same amount of time.

Grilled Courgettes with Garlicky Tahini Yoghurt & Savoury Seed Brittle

This dish of many contrasts is one of my absolute favourite ways to show off versatile courgettes; the cooling yoghurt amplifies their smoky character after a few minutes on the griddle pan, followed by a rest in the grassy fresh marinade. To top things off is a savoury seeded brittle, which you'll want to crumble over everything, or just eat on the go, like the world's best sesame snap.

TIMINGS: 25 MINUTES, PLUS RESTING TIME
SERVES 4

4 courgettes (zucchini)
3 tbsp extra virgin olive oil
1 tbsp red wine vinegar
Juice of 1 lemon
1 garlic clove, bruised with the back of a knife
2 sprigs of oregano, leaves picked
2 sprigs of mint, leaves picked and roughly torn
Salt and pepper

For the garlicky tahini yoghurt
250g (9oz/1 cup) Greek yoghurt
2 garlic cloves, very finely grated or crushed
4 tbsp tahini
Juice of ½ lemon
½ tsp salt
1 tsp honey
Freshly ground pepper

To serve
½ x quantity Savoury Seeded Brittle (see page 185)
Hot flatbreads (optional)
Tomato Braised Green Beans (see page 63 – optional)

Heat a griddle pan over a high heat for at least 5 minutes – you want the pan really hot before adding the courgettes. In the meantime, slice the courgettes lengthways into 1cm (½in) slices. Cook the courgettes in batches so that they don't overcrowd the pan, without moving them around too much so that they turn tender and smoky while forming their distinct black stripes. While the first batch of courgettes is cooking, mix together the remaining ingredients for the courgettes in a mixing bowl. Add a teaspoon of salt and about 10 turns of the pepper mill. Once the courgettes are grilled on one side, turn them with tongs to cook on the other side for a few minutes. Transfer the cooked courgettes to the bowl with the herby oil and toss to coat. Cover immediately with a plate to trap the steam, which will help the courgettes to tenderise and marinade further. Continue to cook the courgettes like this until they're all in the bowl, then set aside to allow the flavours to mingle for half an hour.

Meanwhile, whisk together the ingredients for the tahini yoghurt (make sure the tahini is well-stirred before adding), then taste to check the seasoning. The yoghurt will taste boldly garlicky, but keep in mind that the courgettes and brittle will provide a slightly smoky, sweet and sharp foil for this.

Spread the tahini yoghurt on a wide plate, and top with the courgettes, along with a spoonful of the juices from the bottom of the bowl they were resting in. Sprinkle over some of the brittle to serve.

Serve with hot flatbreads and/or the tomato braised green beans.

Any extra courgettes can be chopped, then stirred through cooked grains, along with fresh herbs, for a filling summery salad.

Variations
Grill and dress green beans as above instead of courgettes, then serve on top of the garlicky yoghurt.

10-Minute Pea & Tahini Soup with Charred Lemon Salsa

This is my version of a soup I heard about from the inspirational Samin Nosrat on her lockdown podcast, *Home Cooking* with Hrishikesh Hirway. I love the fresh, nutty purity of the soup on its own, but the punchy salsa addition transforms its gentle character into something truly memorable and highly repeatable, all in the time it takes to lay the table.

TIMINGS: 10 MINUTES
SERVES 2

For the soup
400ml (14fl oz/1¾ cups)
  vegetable stock
200g (7oz) frozen peas
Leaves from ½ small bunch
  of flatleaf parsley
2 tbsp tahini
Salt and pepper

For the salsa
1 lemon
3 tbsp extra virgin olive oil
4 spring onions (scallions)
1 tbsp flaked (sliced) almonds
¼ tsp cumin seeds
Handful of mint leaves,
  finely chopped
Handful of basil leaves,
  finely chopped

Bring the vegetable stock to the boil in a pan, then stir in the peas and cook for 3 minutes before adding the parsley and tahini. Remove from the heat, cover with a lid and set aside.

Cut the lemon in half around the middle. Squeeze the juice of one half into a small mixing bowl. Slice the pointed end off the other half, so that the juicy flesh is visible. Cut the lemon into transparent, ¼cm (⅛in) slices, picking out the pips as you go. Lay the slices flat on the chopping board and finely chop: pith, skin and all.

Heat the oil in a frying pan over a high heat and when it shimmers, add the chopped lemon, spring onions and a pinch of salt and cook, stirring regularly, for 3 minutes. Add the flaked almonds to the pan and cook for another minute until the spring onions and lemon begin to char and the almonds are turning golden at the edges. Remove from the heat and stir through the cumin seeds, and when they release their fragrance, tip everything into the bowl with the lemon juice. Stir the chopped herbs through the lemon mixture.

Blend the soup, either with a stick blender or jug blender, until smooth. Taste and adjust the seasoning, bearing in mind that the salsa will be tangy and fresh.

Divide the soup between two warm bowls and top with a teaspoon each of the lemon salsa. The soup can be frozen in an airtight container for up to 3 months. Any extra salsa will keep covered in the fridge for up to a week.

Any extra salsa can be used to drizzle over roasted carrots or celeriac (celery root) for a bright lift of flavour, or to dress warm cooked grains or rice.

Variations
Add a handful of spinach along with the parsley for an extra dose of leafy greens.

Raw Asparagus & Lemon Spaghetti

Disclaimer: this calls for spanking fresh asparagus. A good freshness test is whether the spears are firm with tightly closed tips; if they bend easily, it will be impossible to peel them into ribbons, so you'd be better cooking them in 3cm (1¼in) pieces to stir through the pasta instead.

TIMINGS: 30 MINUTES
SERVES 4–6

2 bunches of asparagus
    (about 800g/1¾lb in total)
2 small lemons
6 garlic cloves, finely sliced
Large bunch of parsley (about
    100g/3½oz), leaves and stalks
    separated
500g (1lb 2oz) spaghetti
6 tbsp extra virgin olive oil
¼ tsp dried chilli flakes
Finely grated Parmesan cheese,
    to serve
Salt and pepper

Trim the tough ends from the asparagus by cutting 2cm (¾in) off the base. Trim more if the base of the asparagus feels dry and looks fibrous. Use a vegetable peeler to peel the asparagus spears into thin ribbons into a large bowl.

Fill a large saucepan with water and add a tablespoon of salt. Place on the hob to come to the boil.

Meanwhile, cut 5mm (¼in) off both ends of one of the lemons. Discard the ends and finely slice the trimmed lemon into thin rounds, removing any pips as you go. Very finely chop the lemon rounds, almost to a paste, then set aside in a small bowl with the garlic. Finely chop the parsley stalks and add them to the lemon and garlic.

By now the water for the pasta should have come to the boil. Tip in the spaghetti and cook for 8 minutes, swirling the pasta so it doesn't stick.

While the pasta is cooking, heat 2 tablespoons of the oil in a small frying pan over a medium heat. Add the lemon and garlic mixture to the frying pan, along with the chilli flakes. Fry, stirring occasionally, until the garlic is just beginning to turn golden and the ingredients in the pan are intensely fragrant, about 4 minutes. Roughly chop the parsley leaves. If your asparagus isn't firm or fresh enough to peel into ribbons, add the 3cm (1¼in) pieces of chopped asparagus to the pasta to boil for 3 minutes.

After the pasta has been cooking for 8 minutes, ladle 350ml (12fl oz/1½ cups) of pasta water into a jug. Drain the spaghetti, then immediately return it to the saucepan along with the prepared asparagus, parsley leaves and 250ml (9fl oz/1 cup) of the pasta cooking water. Off the heat, quickly use tongs to turn the asparagus and pasta together until the asparagus loses its perkiness. Add the garlic and lemon mixture to the pasta along with a good grind of pepper and stir to combine. Cut the remaining lemon in half and squeeze over the pasta. The liquid in the pan should create a silky, emulsified looking sauce. If not, add the rest of the pasta cooking water and continue to stir until the pasta looks glossy and creamy.

Divide the pasta between warm bowls and drizzle over the remaining oil. Grate over a generous snowfall of Parmesan just before serving.

Variations
Slice 400g (14oz) mangetout (snowpeas) into ribbons to toss through the pasta instead.

Scorched Cucumbers with Peaches, Herbs & DIY Burrata

I first read about this technique in one of my favourite veg cookbooks (*Ruffage* by Abra Berens). Do follow the steps for the cucumber preparation so that they retain their structure as they cook. This works best with English cucumbers, but other varieties will give the same result (except for bitter cucumbers) and for that reason I've given a cucumber weight for this salad. I've suggested a serving of four as a starter. This works equally well as a main for two alongside the Speedy Spiced Carrot & Quinoa Fritters (see page 141).

TIMINGS: 20 MINUTES,
PLUS 2 HOURS CHILLING TIME
SERVES 4 AS A STARTER OR SIDE

For the DIY burrata
2 x 150g (5½oz) balls Mozzarella
150g (5½oz/scant ⅔ cup) full-fat
    crème fraîche
Salt

For the salad
300g (10½oz) cucumber, roughly cut
    into chunky 3cm (1¼in) pieces
1 red chilli
2 tbsp extra virgin olive oil
1 tbsp rice wine vinegar
1 tsp caster (superfine) sugar
2 ripe peaches, stoned and cut into
    8 wedges
Leaves from ½ small bunch of basil
Leaves from ¼ small bunch of mint
Flaky salt
Black pepper

To serve
1 x quantity Green Herb Oil (see page
    175), or extra virgin olive oil
Crusty bread

Drain the Mozzarella, then tear each ball into 10 pieces. Add to a mixing bowl with the crème fraîche and ¼ teaspoon salt. Stir to combine, then cover and place in the fridge to chill for 2 hours.

Meanwhile, pat the cut sides of the cucumber pieces dry with a piece of kitchen paper. Heat a griddle pan over the highest heat on your hob for at least 5 minutes – you want it to be blazing hot before you start cooking. Char the cucumber pieces for 3 minutes before turning to char for another 2 minutes, without shuffling them about on the griddle – this will help the stripy black char marks to form. Char the chilli for 1 minute on each side too, until it just begins to soften. Remove the cucumber from the griddle pan and place on a chopping board until cool enough to handle. Cut the cucumber pieces in half. Place in a bowl with the olive oil, vinegar, sugar and a pinch of salt. Stir to combine and set aside for 3 minutes.

Arrange the cucumber pieces on a serving platter along with the peach wedges. Remove the stalk from the chilli, and deseed it before finely chopping. Scatter the chilli and herbs over the cucumber and peaches.

When the DIY burrata has had its resting time in the fridge, remove and use a spoon to dot it among the cucumber and peach mixture. Drizzle the Green Herb Oil or olive oil over the salad, then season with flaky salt and freshly ground black pepper.

Serve with crusty bread.

Variations
Char halved little gem (baby bibb) lettuces for 2 minutes on each side before arranging on a platter with the burrata and peaches.

Minty Radish & Broad Bean Salad

Broad beans are a pain to double pod, but they always taste better for it. Frozen broad beans are picked while they're young and tender, and the work of removing them from the hairy pods has already been done. It's for these reasons, as well as the fact that they're available year-round, that I suggest using frozen ones. If using fresh, you'll need about 1.25kg (2¾lb) of broad beans in their pods to yield 300g (10½oz) of podded beans.

TIMINGS: 45 MINUTES
SERVES 2

300g (10½oz) podded broad
  (fava) beans, thawed if frozen
300g (10½oz) radishes
Extra virgin olive oil
2 tsp runny honey
150g (5½oz) quinoa
275ml (9¾oz/scant 1¼ cups)
  vegetable stock
60g (2oz) hard sheep's cheese,
  such as Pecorino
½ x quantity Easy Salsa Verde
  (see page 175)
Handful of fresh mint leaves
Salt and pepper

Preheat the oven to 220°C/425°F/Gas 7.

Bring a saucepan of salted water to the boil. Lower in the broad beans and boil for 3 minutes. Pour the beans into a colander to drain.

Cut all but 50g (1¾oz) of the radishes in half and toss the halved radishes on a roasting tray with enough olive oil to coat. Season with salt and pepper. Roast the radishes for 10 minutes, then remove the tray from the oven and drizzle over the honey. Return the honeyed radishes to the oven for a final 5 minutes until blistered in places and beginning to caramelise.

While the radishes are in the oven, cook the quinoa. Rinse the quinoa in a sieve, then transfer to a saucepan for which you have a lid. Toast the quinoa with a tablespoon of oil over a medium heat for a minute or two, until the quinoa begins to smell nutty and sizzles pleasingly. Pour over the vegetable stock, cover the pan with the lid and bring to the boil. Boil for 5 minutes, then remove the pan from the heat and leave to sit with the lid on, without peeking, for 10 minutes while you continue with the salad.

Slip the broad beans out of their tough white skins. Discard the skins and set the bright green beans aside in a small bowl.

Slice the remaining 50g (1¾oz) of radishes finely into rounds and shave the cheese using a vegetable peeler.

Remove the lid from the quinoa pan and fluff the grains up with a fork. While the quinoa is still warm, pour over the salsa verde and stir to combine. Fold the roasted radishes and broad beans through the salad and transfer to a serving dish. Scatter over the mint leaves, sliced radishes and cheese, and serve immediately.

Any leftovers can be kept covered in the fridge for up to 3 days and make a great addition to pan fried halloumi, grilled fish or tofu.

Variations
Chop green beans into 1cm (½in) pieces and boil in the same way (they won't need peeling).

Spice Marinated Paneer with Chard & Potatoes

Chard is a member of the same family as beetroot, so it can taste earthy without other complementary flavours in the mix. Warming spices are a great foil to its mineral character, and a little creaminess from mild paneer doesn't hurt either. The longer you can leave the cheese to marinate, the better, as it turns more complex in the spice mix.

TIMINGS: 1 HOUR, PLUS OVERNIGHT
MARINATING TIME
SERVES 4

For the paneer
1 tbsp ground cumin
2 tsp ground coriander
1 tsp ground turmeric
½ tsp garlic powder
¼ tsp cayenne pepper
1 tsp salt
250g (9oz) paneer cheese,
   cut into 2cm (¾in) cubes
3 tbsp coconut oil
Salt

For the vegetables
550g (1lb 4oz) potatoes, cut into 2cm
   (¾in) cubes
2 tbsp coconut oil
2 onions, sliced
200g (7oz) bunch of chard, leaves
   and stalks separated
2 garlic cloves, crushed
1 x 400g (14oz) can chickpeas,
   drained
2 tbsp freshly squeezed lemon juice
Leaves from ½ small bunch of
   coriander (cilantro)
Salt and pepper

To serve
Warm naan breads
Plain (full-fat) yoghurt

Variations
Use the same weight of spinach or finely chopped kale instead of chard.

Start by marinating the paneer cheese. Measure the spices into a small mixing bowl and add 1 teaspoon salt. Pierce each cube of paneer all over with the prongs of a fork, then toss to coat in the spice mixture. Cover and marinade in the fridge for up to 24 hours for a more complex flavour. Paneer is a very mild cheese, so the longer it can get to know the spices, the better.

Place the potatoes in a saucepan and cover with cold water. Bring the water to the boil, then parboil the potatoes for 10 minutes. Drain in a colander and allow to steam dry.

Heat the coconut oil for the paneer in a large, deep frying pan over a medium heat. Lift the paneer out of the spice mix, leaving any loose spices in the bowl to use later, and carefully lower into the hot oil. Fry for 10 minutes, tossing the pan occasionally, until the paneer has been cooked on all sides. It should have some hazel patches all over. Lift the paneer out of the pan and transfer to a plate. Set aside.

Heat the coconut oil for the vegetables in the same pan – there's no need to rinse or wash it up. Tip in the potatoes, onions and the spices leftover from marinating the paneer. Stir to combine, and cook over a medium heat for 12–15 minutes, until the potatoes are cooked through.

Finely slice the chard stalks, then transfer to the pan with the potato mixture, along with the garlic. Stir to combine, then when the garlic smells fragrant, add the chickpeas. Half fill the chickpea can with water and tip it into the pan, and sprinkle over a teaspoon of salt. Stir occasionally for the next 5 minutes to cook the chard stalks.

Meanwhile, stack the chard leaves up in batches of three, then roll them up tightly from one side to the other like a Swiss roll. Finely slice the rolls into thin ribbons across the leaves. Add the chard leaves and paneer to the pan, then cover it with a lid and cook for 5 minutes until the leaves are wilted and tender. Squeeze over the lemon juice and scatter the coriander leaves over the vegetables. Stir to combine, then taste and adjust the seasoning.

Serve with warm naan breads and a dollop of yoghurt.

Bitter Leaf Breadcrumb Gratin

On a cold day, this is exactly what I crave: an ambrosial bubbling cheesy bean and herb gratin, spiked with a wake-up call of bitter wedges. The rich sauce makes this a very forgiving recipe – you can use any tightly packed heads of bitter leaves: chicory; round radicchio; or pointed Treviso radicchio. If using round radicchio, you'll need one to two, each cut into eight wedges.

TIMINGS: 1 HOUR
SERVES 4

4 heads red or white chicory, cut into 4 wedges
50g (1¾oz/3½ tbsp) butter, plus extra for greasing
2 tbsp plain white (all-purpose) flour
400ml (14fl oz/1¾ cups) whole milk
1 whole nutmeg
Leaves from 5 sprigs rosemary, picked and chopped
Leaves from ½ small bunch of parsley, chopped
80g (2¾oz) hard cheese, such as Cheddar, Gruyère or Comté, grated
40g (1½oz) blue cheese, such as Stilton, crumbled
1 tsp Dijon mustard
1 x 600g (1lb 5oz) jar butter beans, drained
50g (1¾oz) panko breadcrumbs
30g (1oz) hazelnuts, roughly chopped
Salt and pepper

For the fennel salad
1 fennel bulb, trimmed and very finely sliced
2 celery stalks, very finely sliced at an angle
2 tbsp extra virgin olive oil
30ml (1fl oz/2 tbsp) freshly squeezed lemon juice
Leaves and tender stems from ½ small bunch of parsley

Preheat the oven to 200°C/400°F/Gas 6.

Grease a 20 x 30cm (8 x 12in) baking dish with butter, then nestle the wedges of chicory (or radicchio) tightly in the dish. Dot 20g (⅔oz/1½ tbsp) of the butter over the wedges and season generously with salt and pepper.

Melt the remaining butter in a medium saucepan and when it's bubbling, stir in the flour with a wooden spoon. Cook for a couple of minutes so that the flour loses its rawness. Pour in the milk, stirring continuously to prevent any lumps from forming. Cook for 8–10 minutes over a medium heat, stirring regularly and without letting the mixture boil, until the sauce thickens to the consistency of thick pouring cream. It's done when it clings to the back of a wooden spoon. Remove the sauce from the heat and grate in half the nutmeg, all but a pinch of the rosemary leaves, the parsley, both cheeses (reserving a handful of hard cheese for the topping), mustard and drained beans. Stir to combine and melt the cheese. Season with salt and pepper to taste.

Pour the sauce over the chicory wedges and sprinkle over the breadcrumbs, nuts and reserved cheese and rosemary.

Bake in the oven for 30–35 minutes until the gratin is bubbling at the sides and the top is golden and crisp.

Meanwhile, toss all the ingredients for the salad together and set aside until you're ready to serve.

Allow the gratin to rest out of the oven for 5 minutes before serving alongside the fennel salad.

Variations
Break a large head of cauliflower into small florets to bake in the same way as the bitter wedges.

4

POTATOES

&

CREAMY

ROOTS

These pale roots and tubers are too often relegated to side dishes and supporting acts, so I'm surprised that our deep love for them hasn't elevated their status to hero on the plate. Well, here you are. Potatoes are so much more than chips and roasties (both great, don't get me wrong), and I've drawn from my own experiences growing up as well as some favourite food cultures to highlight their versatility in this chapter.

White Potatoes Today there are about 5,000 varieties of potatoes that are cultivated around the world, but they can loosely be categorised as: 'floury' – higher starch varieties that are good for baking and mashing; 'waxy' – lower starch spuds that hold their shape when boiled, and therefore are better for salads, or sliced on top of casseroles; and 'all-rounders' – which do what they say on the proverbial tin. New potatoes are just potatoes harvested when they are young and small, and need to be cooked quickly to enjoy their flavour and freshness.

Sweet Potatoes (See Sunny Vegetables, page 136) Sweet potatoes and potatoes are only distantly related. The texture and sweet, round-flavoured flesh of sweet potatoes makes them closer to carrots and winter squash in culinary terms.

Parsnips These creamy roots become sweeter the longer they're left in the ground after frosts, and like most hardy vegetables store well for months in a cool, dark place. Ancient Romans believed that parsnips 'prompted men to amatory feelings' (an aphrodisiac!), and I for one, am happy to be their cheerleader, because they're brilliant, if a little uncool these days.

Parsnips are almost as versatile as potatoes – they're fantastic grated into a rösti with crispy edges (see page 90), simmered in coconut milk curries with cashews and lime juice, or roasted with turmeric to serve alongside fluffy rice. I hope the recipes and ideas in this chapter will prompt you to try putting them centre stage, rather than just on the side of a roast.

Cheesy Potato & Shallot Bagels

Potatoes and members of the allium family are both workhorses in the kitchen so it's good to be reminded of how well suited they are. Boiling the potato in its skin prevents the white flesh from becoming waterlogged as it cooks, which ultimately results in a light, fluffy bagel – just be sure not to let the potato cool completely before peeling and mashing, otherwise it will turn dense and gluey.

TIMINGS: 1½ HOURS,
PLUS PROVING TIME
MAKES 8 BAGELS

1 all-rounder potato, such as Desirée (about 250g/9oz), or 250g (9oz) leftover mashed potato
450g (1lb/3¼ cups) strong white bread flour, plus extra for dusting
50g (1¾oz/6 tbsp) wholemeal flour
7g (¼oz) fast acting dried yeast
1 tsp caster (superfine) sugar
150g (5½oz) extra mature Cheddar cheese, grated
2 shallots, finely chopped
1 tsp black onion (nigella) seeds, plus extra for sprinkling
10g (⅓oz/2 tsp) fine salt
Neutral oil, such as mild olive oil, for greasing
Sesame seeds, for sprinkling (optional)
Poppy seeds, for sprinkling (optional)

For poaching
1 tsp bicarbonate of soda (baking soda)
1 tbsp honey

Place the potato in a saucepan and cover with water. Add a generous pinch of salt to the pan. Bring to the boil and cook until a sharp knife passes through the potato easily (about 25–30 minutes). Drain the potato, reserving 210ml (7½fl oz/scant 1 cup) of the cooking water. When the potato is cool enough to handle, but still warm, peel away the skin and discard (this is easiest using your fingers rather than a peeler). In a large mixing bowl, mash the potato until smooth, or pass through a potato ricer. Skip this step if you're cooking with leftover mashed potato, and just measure the correct quantity of mash into a large mixing bowl.

Sift both flours into the bowl with the potato and add the yeast, sugar, cheese, shallots, black onion seeds and salt. Stir to combine, then make a well in the centre and pour in the reserved potato cooking water. Bring the mixture together as a dough in the mixing bowl using clean hands, then transfer to a lightly floured surface and knead for 10–15 minutes until the dough is smooth. This doughy exercise can feel like hard going, but the mixture is more pliable after a brief rest of even a couple of minutes, so I often wander off to open the post or water the plants before continuing to knead. Depending on the potato and the atmosphere, you may need to add a sprinkle more flour here and there if the dough feels particularly sticky. You're looking for it ultimately to have a smooth surface and not to stick to the work surface as you knead. Lightly oil the mixing bowl (there's no need to wash it up) and return the dough to the bowl to prove, covered with a clean tea towel, for an hour in a warm place until doubled in size.

Cut nine squares, 10 x 10cm (4 x 4in) each, of baking parchment and arrange eight of them over two baking trays; place the last one on the kitchen scales to stop the dough from sticking as you weigh it. Divide the dough into eight balls, using scales to measure roughly 140g (5oz) each, and divide among the parchment squares, spacing them 3cm (1¼in) apart. Using a lightly floured finger, poke a hole in the centre of one of the dough balls and make a pointy circular motion to create a hole, 1cm (½in) in diameter in the middle, using the parchment for purchase. If you're feeling confident, you could spin the ring in the air like an Italian making pizza dough. Repeat with the remaining dough balls, then cover the trays with tea towels and leave to prove again for an hour at room temperature.

Preheat the oven to 200°C/400°C/Gas 6.

Fill a large saucepan with 2 litres (70fl oz/8¼ cups) of water and bring to a gentle simmer. Add the bicarbonate of soda and honey to the pan. Peel the parchment away and drop the first bagel into the simmering water. Cook for 30 seconds, during which time it should bob up to the surface, before using a slotted spoon to flip it over and cook for another 30 seconds on the other side. Lift the bagel out of the water with the slotted spoon and return to the baking sheet on its piece of parchment. Repeat with the remaining dough balls, poaching batches of two or three bagels in the pan at a time.

Once all the bagels are poached, sprinkle their surfaces with black onion seeds and sesame and poppy seeds, if using.

Bake in the oven for 25–28 minutes until deep golden. Transfer the cooked bagels to a cooling rack to cool completely. They're best eaten within a couple of days of being cooked, but they freeze well for up to 3 months.

Serve the bagels spread with a thick layer of cream cheese and your favourite savoury additions (a crispy fried egg; chopped capers and dill; and anchovies and cucumbers are all excellent additions).

Variations
Replace the potato with puréed parsnip and add some finely chopped rosemary.

Melt in the Middle Potato Cakes with Mustardy Greens

Taleggio is an unctuous, buttery cheese from Northern Italy that melts like chocolate. It really is the secret ingredient here, so try to seek it out in larger supermarkets or cheesemongers if you can. The cakes will hold their shape better once the potatoes are cool, so don't be tempted to rush the chilling steps.

TIMINGS: 1 HOUR,
PLUS CHILLING TIME
SERVES 4

For the potato cakes
1kg (2lb 4oz) floury potatoes, such as
   Maris Piper, peeled and cut into
   3cm (1¼in) chunks
Bunch of spring onions (scallions),
   finely sliced
1 tsp finely chopped rosemary
5 tbsp rice flour
Sunflower oil, for greasing
125g (4½oz) Taleggio cheese, cut into
   8 cubes
50g (1¾oz/⅓ cup) quick cook polenta
Salt and pepper

For the mustardy greens
200g (7oz) kale or spring greens,
   tough stalks removed and leaves
   roughly torn
1 tbsp butter
1 tbsp extra virgin olive oil
1 heaped tsp Dijon mustard
1 tsp red wine vinegar

Place the potato chunks in a large saucepan, cover with water and salt generously. Cover with a lid and bring to the boil, then simmer for 15–20 minutes, until the potatoes are soft throughout to the point of a sharp knife. Drain the potatoes in a colander, then transfer to a mixing bowl and mash while still hot.

Add the spring onions, rosemary and rice flour to the bowl and mix to combine, then season with salt and pepper. Lay a piece of baking parchment on a large roasting tray and grease lightly with oil.

Allow the potato mixture to cool to room temperature. Scoop out 100g (3½oz) of the mixture and flatten it out to fit on your palm, then place a cube of Taleggio in the centre. Press the potato mixture around the cheese to seal, then form into a disc, roughly 2cm (¾in) thick. Spread the polenta onto a plate and dip the potato cake into the polenta to cover. Place the potato cake onto the prepared roasting tray, press down with your hand gently to flatten without bursting and repeat with the remaining mixture to form eight potato cakes. Transfer to the fridge to chill for 30 minutes. (At this point the potato cakes can be frozen for up to 3 months. Allow an extra 8 minutes of cooking time in the oven.)

Preheat the oven to 220°C/425°F/Gas 7.

Cook the potato cakes on the middle shelf in the oven for 25 minutes, turning the tray halfway through cooking.

Meanwhile, rinse the prepared greens in a colander and transfer to a deep frying pan, set over a medium heat. Cover the pan with a lid and cook for 2–3 minutes until the leaves are bright green and tender – they should steam in the water that clings to the leaves after they've been rinsed. Remove the lid and stir through the butter and oil. Turn the heat up to high and stir regularly for a couple of minutes until all the liquid has evaporated from the pan. Add the mustard and vinegar, stir to combine, then season well with salt and pepper to taste. Remove from the heat and divide the greens between four warm plates, alongside a couple of potato cakes per person.

Little Pea & Potato Samosas

This is the kind of food that doesn't need much attention once you've served it – it sits well for a while and can be largely made in advance. The combination of zingy cabbage slaw and spicy, piping hot pastries is party food perfection to me.

TIMINGS: 1 HOUR
SERVES 4–6

For the samosas
300g (10½oz) new potatoes, cut into rough 1.5cm (⅝in) chunks
Coconut oil, for frying and brushing
Bunch of spring onions (scallions), finely sliced
5cm (2in) piece ginger, peeled and grated
2 garlic cloves, grated
1 tsp cumin seeds
½ tsp ground turmeric
½ tsp fennel seeds
½ tsp black mustard seeds
½ tsp ground coriander
75g (2½oz) frozen peas
Stems from 1 large bunch (100g/3½oz) of coriander (cilantro)
6 sheets filo (phyllo) pastry
Salt and pepper
Cumin or black onion (nigella) seeds, to decorate

For the red cabbage salad
400g (14oz) red cabbage, finely sliced
40ml (1½fl oz/2½ tbsp) freshly squeezed lime juice (1–2 limes)
30g (1oz) roasted peanuts, roughly chopped
100g (3½oz) pomegranate seeds (arils)
Salt

To serve
1 x quantity Coriander Chutney (see page 176)

Fill a saucepan with water and bring to the boil. Lower in the potato chunks and bring the water to the boil again. Boil for 8 minutes, until the potatoes are tender to the point of a sharp knife. Drain and allow to steam dry in a colander.

Meanwhile, add the red cabbage, lime juice and ½ teaspoon of salt to a small bowl and rub together until it turns bright purple. Stir through the peanuts and pomegranate and set aside until ready to serve.

Heat a couple of tablespoons of coconut oil in a large frying pan over a medium heat and add the spring onions. Cook, stirring regularly for 3 minutes, until the spring onions have softened. Add the ginger and garlic and cook for another minute until fragrant, then stir in the spices. When you hear the mustard seeds start to pop, stir through the potatoes and peas and cook until the peas are just tender. Roughly chop the coriander stems, then add them to the pan and remove from the heat. Season well with salt and pepper.

Preheat the oven to 180°C/350°F/Gas 4 and line a couple of baking sheets with baking parchment.

Unroll the filo and, in a stack, cut the sheets lengthways into three evenly sized strips. Keep the pile of filo covered with a clean tea towel while you fold each samosa. Melt 3 tablespoons of coconut oil in a small saucepan. Take a strip of filo and brush all over with oil. Take a heaped dessertspoon of the potato mixture and spoon onto the pastry at the end of the strip closest to you with a filo 'tail' facing away from you. Take the right-hand bottom corner of the pastry and fold it up to meet the left side of the pastry and make a triangle. Continue to fold in a triangle shape until the pastry is used up, then brush with oil to seal. Decorate with black onion or cumin seeds. Repeat with the remaining pastry and filling. At this stage the filled samosas can be frozen in an airtight container between layers of baking parchment for up to 3 months. Place the samosas onto the prepared baking sheets and bake for 20 minutes until flaky and golden all over. If cooking from frozen, add another 8 minutes cooking time.

Serve the samosas alongside the salad and Coriander Chutney.

Creamy New Potato & Charred Corn Chowder

When I first cooked this recipe, my mum was looking after my son Fyfe and we both inhaled two bowls in about 10 minutes. As a family (pre-Fyfe), we spent eight years on the East coast in the US where creamy chowders are served as comfort food; they're rich, humble and sustaining, made from the land (potatoes, pork) and often sea, too (clams and white fish are common). For Americans who live on the windy North East coast, 'The Chowder' is a comforting constant. My version doesn't contain pork, but it does have plenty of smoulder from charred corn and smoked paprika.

TIMINGS: 45 MINUTES
SERVES 4

3 tbsp mild olive oil
2 onions, finely chopped
1 celery stick, finely chopped,
    leaves (if any) reserved
2 green chillies, finely chopped
2 garlic cloves, finely chopped
2 bay leaves
1 tsp sweet smoked paprika
500g (1lb 2oz) new potatoes,
    cut into rough 2cm (¾in) chunks
600ml (21fl oz/2½ cups) vegetable
    stock
150g (5½oz) can sweetcorn, or 2 ears
    sweetcorn, kernels removed
1 tsp coriander seeds
150ml (5½fl oz/scant ⅔ cup) double
    (heavy) cream
Small bunch of parsley, leaves and
    tender stems only
Small bunch of coriander (cilantro),
    leaves and tender stems only
Juice of 1 lemon
2 tbsp Crispy Fried Shallots
    (see page 181)
Salt and pepper

Heat 2 tablespoons of the oil in a large saucepan over a medium heat. Add the onions, celery and a pinch of salt and plenty of freshly ground black pepper. Cook, stirring occasionally for 10 minutes, until the vegetables are soft and translucent. Add the chilli, garlic and bay leaves and cook for another minute until fragrant. Stir the paprika and potatoes into the pan and when everything is sizzling after a minute, pour the vegetable stock over. Bring the pan to the boil, then turn it down to a very gentle simmer. Cook for 10 minutes until the potato pieces are tender enough to eat, but not near the point of collapse.

Meanwhile, drain and pat the sweetcorn dry (if using canned) between layers of kitchen paper. Heat the remaining oil in a small frying pan over a high heat and add the sweetcorn and coriander seeds. Cook, stirring occasionally for 6–8 minutes. During this time, the sweetcorn will pop and blister. Remove from the heat when the sweetcorn is charred in places.

Back to the potatoes. Remove half of the vegetables and liquid from the saucepan and transfer to a blender, or jug for which you have a stick blender. Blend until smooth, then return the puréed mixture to the saucepan along with the charred sweetcorn and cream. Roughly chop three quarters of the herbs and add them to the saucepan too. Simmer for 5 minutes, then remove the pan from the heat and squeeze in the juice of half the lemon. Taste the chowder, and add more lemon juice, salt or pepper to taste.

Ladle the chowder into warm bowls and top with the remaining herbs, Crispy Fried Shallots and any reserved celery leaves.

Variations
Use half a bulb of fennel with fronds instead of the celery. Finely slice the fennel bulbs and reserve a few fronds to decorate the chowder as it's served.

Sharing Parsnip Rösti with Chilli Spiked Tomato Sauce

The natural sweetness in parsnip is crying out for a hit of sharp acidity, and a tangy dressed salad would work well if you wanted to serve the rösti as a side dish instead. Typically a parsnip rösti would need an egg to bind it and plenty of oil to crisp as it cooks – but I've gone one step further and folded mayonnaise (an egg and oil emulsion) through the mixture for a decadent rösti.

TIMINGS: 45 MINUTES,
PLUS DRAINING TIME
SERVES 4

For the rösti
500g (1lb 2oz) parsnips, peeled
200g (7oz) potato, peeled
1 onion
100g (3½oz) Gruyère cheese, grated
2 tbsp rosemary leaves,
    roughly chopped
1 tbsp mayonnaise
1 egg
Salt and pepper

For the chilli spiked tomato sauce
2 tbsp extra virgin olive oil
2 garlic cloves, sliced
2 bay leaves
¼ tsp chilli flakes
1 x 400g (14oz) can chopped
    tomatoes
10 green olives, pitted and roughly
    chopped
⅛ whole nutmeg, grated

For the sage leaves
Mild olive oil, for frying
1 small bunch of sage, leaves picked
Flaky salt

Variations

You can grate other root vegetables into the rösti mixture, such as swede and celeriac, but you'll need to keep the same weight of potato as the starch in the spuds helps the rösti to hold together.

Grate the parsnips, potato and onion into a large mixing bowl. Scatter over 2 teaspoons of salt, toss to combine, then cover with a clean, damp tea towel and set aside for 30 minutes. This rest period draws out liquid from the vegetables, helping them to turn crisp as they cook.

Preheat the oven to 180°C/350°F/Gas 4.

Tip the salted vegetables into a clean, dry tea towel and gather up the sides. Squeeze the ball of vegetables tightly five or six times to extract as much liquid as you can. Tip the vegetables back into the same bowl, then stir through the cheese, rosemary, mayonnaise and egg.

Heat enough oil in a 20cm (8in) oven-proof frying pan (non-stick if you have it) to cover the base of the pan. Pack the parsnip mixture into the pan, pressing it in tightly with a spatula. Fry over a medium heat until it's sizzling and beginning to colour around the outside. Place on the middle shelf in the oven to continue to cook for 25 minutes.

While the rösti is in the oven, make the sauce. Heat the olive oil in a small saucepan over a medium heat and add the garlic. Cook for a minute until sizzling and golden in places, but not yet brown, then add the bay leaves and chilli, followed by the chopped tomatoes. Season well with salt and pepper and simmer until the tomato has turned a deep, rich red and the sauce has thickened – about 20 minutes. Stir in the olives and nutmeg and simmer for a couple of minutes more, then remove from the heat.

Remove the rösti from the oven and allow to cool for 10 minutes while you fry the sage leaves. Lay a sheet of kitchen paper over a cooling rack and place next to the hob. In another small frying pan, heat enough oil to cover the base of the pan by 2mm (⅟₁₆in) over a medium–high heat. When ripples form in the oil after 45 seconds or so, tip in the sage leaves and fry, stirring with a slotted spoon, until the leaves begin to curl and turn crisp. Listen for the sizzling to stop. Lift the leaves out of the hot oil onto the kitchen paper and sprinkle immediately with flaky salt.

Invert the rösti onto a plate and scatter with crispy sage leaves. Slice into wedges and serve with the tomato sauce.

Potato Gnocchi with Bright Red Vodka Sauce

This happy marriage is loosely inspired by both pasta alla vodka and a gnocchi di patate with tomato sauce. I use a combination of tomatoes and peppers for layers of brightness alongside the fresh green herbs. Why vodka? As well as sharpening the flavours of every fresh ingredient, it adds a touch of heat and balances out the sweetness of the fruitier flavours in the most enchanting way.

TIMINGS: 1 HOUR,
PLUS RESTING TIME
SERVES 4–6

1kg (2lb 4oz) floury potatoes, such as King Edward
150g–175g (5½–6oz/1 cup plus 2 tbsp–1 ⅓ cups) Italian 00 flour, plus extra for dusting
¼ whole nutmeg
40g (1½oz/2½ tbsp) unsalted butter, for frying
Salt and pepper
Grated Parmesan cheese, to serve (optional)

For the sauce
400g (14oz) cherry tomatoes
200g (7oz) jarred roasted red peppers
2 garlic cloves
½ small bunch of basil
½ small bunch of tarragon
50g (1¾oz/3½ tbsp) unsalted butter
50ml (1¾fl oz/3½ tbsp) vodka
100ml (3½fl oz/scant ½ cup) double (heavy) cream
¼ whole nutmeg

Place the unpeeled potatoes in a large saucepan and cover with cold water. Add a couple of teaspoons of salt to the pan, then place the pan over a high heat with the lid on. Bring to the boil, then continue to boil for 25 minutes, until the potatoes are soft throughout to the point of a sharp knife. Drain the potatoes in a colander, then when they're cool enough to handle (for my asbestos hands, this is after about 5 minutes or so), quickly scrape off the skins using a blunt knife. Transfer the potatoes to a large mixing bowl or potato ricer and mash until smooth. If you spot any solid lumps, continue to mash until smooth, or pass the potatoes through a fine mesh sieve using the back of a wooden spoon to press the potatoes through the holes.

Scatter 150g (5½oz/1 cup plus 2 tbsp) of the flour on a clean work surface. Crumble the mashed potatoes over the top of the flour and grate over half the nutmeg. Bring the dough and flour together using lightly floured hands. You might need to add the remaining flour to bring the dough together if it's very shaggy, or sticky. Once the flour is incorporated and the dough holds together as one ball after 2–3 minutes of kneading, cover the dough with the bowl used to mash the potatoes and rest for half an hour.

While the dough is resting, make the sauce. Place the tomatoes, peppers, garlic and herbs in the bowl of a food processor with a ½ teaspoon of salt. Blitz until smooth. Melt the butter in a small saucepan over a medium heat until bubbling and use a spatula to transfer all of the red sauce from the food processor to the saucepan. Bring the mixture to a simmer and continue to cook gently for 25 minutes.

Divide the potato dough into four portions, then use lightly floured hands to roll each portion into a rope, rocking the dough back and forth from the centre outwards until it's roughly 2cm (¾in) thick. Use a blunt knife or dough scraper to cut each rope into 2cm (¾in) pieces. Dip your thumb in flour, then press into the centre of each potato piece to create little gnocchi that look like a cross between an unbaked thumbprint cookie, and very thick orecchiette.

Bring a large saucepan of water to the boil, and salt the water well. While the water is heating up, melt the butter for frying the gnocchi in a large frying pan over a low–medium heat. When the water in the saucepan is at a rolling boil, lower in half of the gnocchi and cook until they rise to the surface of the water. Use a slotted spoon or spider strainer to lift them out of the water and into the buttery pan. Repeat with the remaining gnocchi, occasionally stirring the boiled gnocchi in the butter to prevent them from sticking. Keep the gnocchi warm over a low heat. Any extra uncooked gnocchi can be frozen in an airtight container between layers of baking parchment for up to 3 months. If cooking the gnocchi from frozen, allow an extra 30 seconds cooking time once they rise to the surface (test one to check it's hot throughout).

Add the vodka and cream to the pan with the tomato and pepper sauce and simmer for a couple of minutes. Grate in a generous dusting of fresh nutmeg. Pour the sauce over the gnocchi and stir to combine. Taste and add salt and pepper according to your preference.

Spoon the saucy gnocchi into warm bowls and serve immediately, with grated Parmesan if you like.

Variations
Grill your own red peppers (see page 120), or use the same weight of tinned tomatoes instead.

5

TOUGHER

TO LOVE

ROOTS

The vegetables in this chapter have a coarse reputation, often associated with times of hardship. For those with a weekly veg box delivery, it's never the delicate greens or juicy tomatoes that languish week after week: without fail it's the swede, beetroot and celeriac. These fruits of the earth might be tougher to love than those which grow above ground, but using the right techniques they're marvellous, and don't deserve their lowly position on the hierarchy of favoured vegetables.

Beetroot Generally, the darker the colour of the beetroot, the more earthy and complex it will taste. Yellow and white-fleshed varieties won't stain your fingers (or wooden boards) as you prepare them. Beetroot can be eaten raw or cooked, but some people find the oxalic acid in the raw roots causes irritation in their throats. The leaves can be eaten too, and cooked in the same way as you would chard. Look for smooth, plump beetroots that feel heavy for their size. Lots of pock marks or discolouration is a sign of age or pests.

Turnips & Swede (Rutabaga) These roots are members of the brassica family – the same tree that includes cabbage and broccoli – and their flavour contains the characteristic hot, sulphuric bite. Both can be stored for months if kept properly like other roots, in a cool, dark place. The pleasant pepperiness of these roots is an ideal match for butter, cheese and black pepper.

Celeriac (Celery Root) There's no doubt that this knobbly root has an intimidating appearance, with a face that only a mother could love. For this reason, I'm unusually ruthless when I peel it, preferring long swathes of a sharp knife over a peeler, which struggles with the troughs and tendrils. Celeriac and celery share that same special flavour, which can be a revelation when paired with acidic and salty accents like capers or cheese.

Jerusalem Artichokes (Sunchokes) Even though they have a pale, creamy flesh, the flavour of Jerusalem artichokes is far from neutral, and is in fact very distinctive – almost like chestnuts when raw, and more sweet and reminiscent of globe artichokes when cooked. They can cause noisy digestive repercussions in some, but they're full of good fibre and are meant to be great for gut health.

Spiced Root Vegetable & Lime Pancakes

The batter in this recipe is made from a combination of chickpea and plain flour, which as well as being a good source of protein (from the ground chickpeas), cooks into a deliciously nutty and complex tasting pancake the longer the batter is left to rest. It's inspired by the thin, lacy dosas – fermented pancakes – from South India. As a vehicle for the spicy vegetables the pancakes are excellent, and I enjoy the flavour and texture contrasts that a jumble of root vegetables offers. This will serve four generously.

TIMINGS: 45 MINUTES,
PLUS RESTING TIME
SERVES 4

For the pancake batter
225g (8oz/2¼ cups) gram (chickpea) flour
100g (3½oz/¾ cup) plain white (all-purpose) flour
¼ tsp bicarbonate of soda (baking soda)
1 tsp ground turmeric
1 tsp cumin seeds
1 tsp salt

For the filling
100g (3½oz) frozen peas
750g (1lb 10oz) mix of celeriac (celery root), swede (rutabaga), new potatoes and Jerusalem artichokes (sunchokes)
Coconut oil, for frying
2 onions, roughly chopped
2 green chillies, finely chopped
2 garlic cloves, finely chopped
5cm (2in) piece fresh ginger, peeled and grated
2 tsp cumin seed
1 tsp coriander seed
1 tsp mustard seed
1 tsp ground turmeric
Small bunch of coriander (cilantro), leaves and tender stems only
2 limes
Salt

To serve
Natural yoghurt
Mango chutney (optional)

Start by mixing together the ingredients for the pancake batter. Sift both flours and the bicarbonate of soda into a large mixing bowl. Stir through the spices, then make a well in the centre, pour in 550ml (19fl oz/scant 2½ cups) warm water and whisk until no dry patches or lumps are visible and the batter is smooth. Cover the bowl with a clean tea towel and set aside for up to 24 hours, or at least while you cook the filling. The longer the batter rests, the more complex the flavour will be, so I often like to make the batter in the morning, or even the night before, in anticipation of a more delicious pancake to fill.

Measure the peas into a bowl and set aside to defrost. Fill a large saucepan with well salted water and place on the hob to come to the boil. Peel and cut the vegetables into roughly 1½cm (⅝in) pieces. Lower the root vegetables into the boiling water and cook for 8–10 minutes until the pieces are easily pierced with the sharp point of a knife. Because you're using a selection of root vegetables, they'll have varying tenderness at this stage, but that's all part of the fun. Remove the pan from the heat and tip the vegetables into a colander to steam dry.

Melt a couple of tablespoons of coconut oil in a large non-stick frying pan over a medium heat. Add the onions and a pinch of salt and cook, stirring occasionally, until the onions have softened, about 8–10 minutes. Stir in the chillies, garlic and ginger, and cook for a minute more until sizzling and fragrant. Add the dried spices and stir to toast them for another minute before stirring in the root vegetables. Add a pinch of salt and turn the heat up to medium–high. Stirring regularly, continue to cook the mixture in the pan until everything is piping hot and the root vegetables are beginning to brown in places, about 8 minutes. Stir through the peas, then scrape the filling into a bowl and keep warm in a low oven while you cook the pancakes.

Preheat the oven to 150°C/300°F/Gas 2. Wipe out the frying pan with a clean tea towel and add a couple of tablespoons of coconut oil to melt over a medium heat. Whisk the salt into the pancake batter, then pour in roughly half of the coconut oil from the pan into the batter. Mix to combine, then pour a ladleful of the batter into the centre of the pan. Tilt the pan to distribute the batter thinly and evenly – the edges don't need to be perfectly round. Cook for 2–3 minutes on one side until the surface of the pancake looks dry and the pancake perimeter easily lifts when teased with a spatula. Flip to cook the other side for another minute. Repeat with the remaining batter, adding more oil if the pancakes begin to burn. Keep the cooked pancakes warm in the oven while you ladle out and cook the remaining batter.

Roughly chop the coriander and stir three-quarters through the vegetable mixture. Squeeze the juice of one of the limes over the vegetables, then cut the other lime into wedges.

To serve, place a pancake on each plate and spoon a generous serving spoon of the filling into the centre. Top with a few coriander leaves and a squeeze of lime and drizzle over the yoghurt. Have the remaining pancakes in a stack and the vegetable filling in a bowl on the table for second helpings. Everyone is different, but I like the sweetness of gently spiced mango chutney alongside the sharp lime-dressed vegetables.

Variations

Steam cubed potatoes until tender, then cook in the same manner as the root vegetables.

Lemony Celeriac & Fennel Comfort Soup

I spent a big portion of my childhood in the US, where a series of short stories 'to open the heart and rekindle the spirit' in a collection of books called *Chicken Soup for the Soul* were sold in every coffee shop and gas station. Healing chicken soup has just never been something we cooked at home because we had our own comfort food traditions (shepherd's pie, obviously). This cosy and bright soup has the same nurturing impact.

TIMINGS: 50 MINUTES
SERVES 6

400g (14oz) celeriac (celery root)
4 tbsp extra virgin olive oil
1 large fennel bulb (about 400g/14oz), cut into 1cm (½in) dice
2 onions, roughly chopped
1–2 lemons
4 garlic cloves, crushed
2 bay leaves
100g (3½oz) orzo, or other tiny pasta shape
1.75 litres (60fl oz/7¾ cups) vegetable stock
Salt and pepper

To serve
6 tbsp double (heavy) cream
2 stalks dill, leaves picked
Crunchy Chilli Oil (see page 182 – optional)

Variations

Replace the celeriac in this soup with 2 stalks of finely sliced celery and 400g (14oz) of peeled, waxy potatoes, cut into 1.5cm (⅝in) cubes. Cook the celery and potato for the same time as you would the celeriac.

Roughly peel the celeriac with a large knife, cutting away any gritty roots and shoots – these bits aren't worth excavating. Peeling with a sharp knife might feel a bit cavalier, but compared to most root vegetables with smooth, round skins, celeriac tends to be full of crevices and craters, so a peeler can get stuck, whereas a sharp knife slices away problem areas with little resistance. Chop the celeriac into rough, 1cm (½in) cubes.

Heat the olive oil in a large saucepan over a medium–high heat. Add the celeriac, fennel, onions and 2 teaspoons of salt, along with a generous grind of black pepper. Cook the vegetables, stirring occasionally, for 25–30 minutes until they're all beginning to caramelise and the celeriac has lost its rigid edges. The key to the flavour of this soup is the sweet vegetables, which contrast with the sharp lemon, so taste to check the flavour of the vegetables and continue to cook and develop the sugars if they're still fibrous and at all bitter.

Peel the skin from one of the lemons, then chop as finely as you can. Add this to the vegetables along with the garlic and bay leaves and stir for a couple of minutes until fragrant. Stir in the orzo and vegetable stock and cook for 6–8 minutes, until the orzo is tender.

Squeeze 50ml (1¾fl oz/3½ tbsp) of juice from the lemons and pour into the soup. Taste the soup and add more salt if you prefer.

Ladle the soup into warm bowls and add a tablespoon of cream to each. Scatter dill leaves over the top and swirl in a drizzle of chilli oil.

Once the soup is cooked, the orzo will continue to release its starch, thickening the soup the longer it sits, so it's best eaten straightaway. If you're making the soup ahead of time, it's best to make it up to the stage where you add the orzo, then cook the pasta just before you're ready to serve. Any extra soup can be reheated, but will need to be thinned down with hot vegetable stock.

Herby Swede & Gruyère Cake

The humble swede ('neep' if you're Scottish) has been a stalwart in our kitchens for centuries and a crucial ingredient in some Great British dishes. It also has A Bad Reputation for being uninspiring and worthy. Swede needs some TLC to bring out its sweet and bitter charms (and a generous touch with fat). This savoury cake makes a great supper, still warm from the oven with herby new potatoes and salad, or as part of a lunchbox or buffet-style spread. It's pretty and portable, and is good hot or at room temperature.

TIMINGS: 1¾ HOURS
SERVES 6

100g (3½oz/7 tbsp) unsalted butter, plus extra for greasing
1 medium swede (rutabaga) (about 650g/1lb 7oz), peeled and cut into 1cm (½in) cubes
4 small shallots, finely sliced
200g (7oz/1½ cups) plain white (all-purpose) flour
1 tsp baking powder
Bunch of spring onions (scallions), finely sliced
1 tbsp roughly chopped rosemary leaves
175g (6oz/⅔ cup) Greek yoghurt
6 eggs
150g (5½oz) Gruyère cheese, grated
Small bunch of parsley
2 tsp black onion (nigella) seeds
Salt and pepper
Chutney and salad, to serve

Preheat the oven to 200°C/400°F/Gas 6.

Line the base of a 23cm (9in) springform tin with baking parchment and grease the sides liberally with butter.

Cut the butter into 1cm (½in) cubes and toss with the swede, shallots and a generous pinch each of salt and pepper in the prepared tin. Wrap foil around the base and the sides of the tin, then place it in the oven to roast for half an hour, removing it every 10 minutes to turn the vegetables in the melted butter. Check the swede after this time with a sharp knife – if it's not tender, cover the tin with foil and continue to cook for another 8–10 minutes until it is.

Meanwhile, sift the flour into a large mixing bowl with the baking powder. Add the spring onions and rosemary and stir to combine. In a separate bowl, whisk together the yoghurt, eggs and cheese to combine. Pick out three attractive whole parsley stems and set aside. Roughly chop the remaining parsley leaves and tender stems and stir into the egg and cheese mixture with the black onion seeds. Season the wet ingredients with ¾ teaspoon of salt and a few turns of the pepper mill, then add the dry ingredients to the bowl with the wet and fold with a spatula until combined.

Remove the swede from the oven and turn the temperature down to 180°C/350°F/Gas 4. Pour the batter over the swede, then return to the oven to bake for 5 minutes. Remove the cake tin from the oven and arrange the reserved parsley stems artistically on top of the cake. Press down slightly if the cake has started to dry on the surface. Return to the oven to bake for 30 minutes, until the batter is set and a skewer inserted into the centre comes out clean. Allow the cake to cool in the tin for 10 minutes before releasing.

Slice the cake into wedges before serving warm or at room temperature with chutney and salad. Once cool, the cake can be stored in an airtight container in the fridge for up to 3 days. Allow to come to room temperature, or warm gently, before serving.

Variations
Replace the swede with celeriac (celery root), which will roast in the same time.

Cosy Jerusalem Artichoke Risotto

If you're familiar with the windy effects that Jerusalem artichokes (sunchokes) can have on the digestive system, then I imagine you're smiling at the conscious inclusion of 'cosy' in the recipe title. For this risotto I use the vegetable bouillon that comes in tubs; if you're using a stock cube, break it in half to dissolve in the hot water and add more seasoning to taste.

TIMINGS: 45 MINUTES
SERVES 4–6

75g (2½oz/5 tbsp) unsalted butter
2 tbsp extra virgin olive oil
1 onion, finely chopped
1 carrot, peeled and finely chopped
½ fennel, finely chopped
300g (10½oz) Jerusalem artichokes (sunchokes)
4 garlic cloves, crushed
2 bay leaves
Bunch of thyme, tied tightly with string
400g (14oz/scant 2 cups) carnaroli risotto rice
200ml (7fl oz/generous ¾ cup) dry white wine
1.5 litres (52fl oz/6½ cups) hot very weak vegetable stock
100g (3½oz) extra mature Cheddar cheese, finely grated
40g (1½oz) hazelnuts, roughly chopped
Salt and pepper
1 lemon, cut into wedges, to serve

Melt 25g (1oz) of the butter with the olive oil in a large saucepan over a medium heat. When sizzling, tip in the onion, carrot and fennel and add 1 teaspoon salt. Cook, stirring occasionally, for 12–15 minutes, until the vegetables are soft and sweet.

After this time, prepare the Jerusalem artichokes. Peel half of the Jerusalem artichokes and cut them into 2cm (¾in) cubes. Add them to the vegetables in the hot pan as you go because they can discolour quickly. Scrub the other half, don't peel them, and set aside.

Stir the garlic and herbs into the vegetable mixture in the pan and cook for a minute until fragrant. Stir in the rice, moving it around constantly for a minute. Add the wine and stir until it has all been absorbed (about a minute). Maintaining the heat so that the rice constantly bubbles confidently, but not furiously, add the stock a ladleful at a time until the rice is plump and creamy, stirring after each addition. This should take no longer than 18 minutes. The perfect risotto is saucy rather than sturdy, so be confident when you're happy that it's *al dente*. If the risotto feels stodgy when you stir it, add a ladleful more stock and stir for a minute before removing from the heat. Add 25g (1oz) more of the butter and two-thirds of the cheese and beat for 30 seconds. Remove the pan from the heat, cover with a lid and push to the back of the hob to relax and keep warm.

Heat the remaining butter in a small frying pan over a medium heat. Slice the remaining Jerusalem artichokes into 5mm (¼in) rounds and add them to the buttery pan with a pinch of salt. Cook for a couple of minutes before adding the hazelnuts. Fry, stirring regularly, for 10 minutes until the Jerusalem artichokes are golden and tender.

Spoon the risotto into warm bowls, removing the herbs as you go, and top with the Jerusalem artichoke mixture and the remaining grated Cheddar. Serve with the lemon wedges.

The risotto is best eaten immediately, but any extra can be rolled into balls and breadcrumbed before being transformed into arancini either in a very hot oven or very hot frying oil. It's up to you whether you choose to stuff them with more cheese, but I know which side of the fence I'm on.

Variations

Replace the Jerusalem artichokes with the same weight of celeriac (celery root), cutting into 1cm (½in) cubes to fry with the butter and hazelnuts.

Fresh Beetroot &
Green Olive Bucatini

I'm sometimes guilty of choosing beetroot's leafy cousins (chard, spinach) over the earthy root because they help to get dinner on the table quickly. This dish, however, starts with grated beetroot, which cooks in minutes to create a striking magenta sauce, punctuated with salty olives and fresh mint and lemon. Be generous with the green oil and drizzle over more than you normally would, as the savouriness and crunchy bits elevate every bite.

TIMINGS: 30 MINUTES
SERVES 2 GENEROUSLY

For the bucatini
Bunch of spring onions (scallions)
5 tbsp extra virgin olive oil
250g (9oz) raw beetroot (about 2 medium), peeled and grated
200g (7oz) bucatini pasta
15 pitted green olives in brine
15g (½oz) mint, leaves roughly chopped
Juice of 1 lemon
75g (2½oz) fresh goats' or feta cheese
Salt and pepper

For the green onion oil
6 tbsp extra virgin olive oil
1 tsp black onion (nigella) seeds

Trim the base and any discoloured leaves from the spring onions. Finely slice the white and light green parts and set the darker green ends aside for the green oil. Heat 2 tablespoons of the olive oil in a wide frying pan over a medium heat. Add the beetroot and a pinch of salt and fry, stirring regularly, for a few minutes until the beetroot releases plenty of steam and softens. Stir in the sliced spring onions and plenty of cracked pepper – more than you think you need. Fry for a couple of minutes until the spring onions have softened, then turn the heat off and stir in the remaining olive oil and add the bucatini, breaking the noodles in half if they don't fit in the pan. Roughly chop the olives and add to the pan with 3 tablespoons of brine from the jar, a generous pinch of salt and one-quarter of the mint.

Fill and boil the kettle, and turn the heat back on under the beetroot pan. Pour 700ml (24fl oz/3 cups) of water over the pasta and beetroot mixture and stir to combine. Bring to the boil, then cook, stirring often, for 7 minutes, or until the pasta is cooked through and a rich, magenta sauce has formed.

While the bucatini is cooking, make the green onion oil. Lay a sheet of kitchen paper over a cooling rack and set by the hob. Finely slice the green spring onion tips as finely as you can. Heat the olive oil in a small saucepan over a medium–high heat. After 30 seconds, drop a piece of spring onion into the oil. If it sizzles straightaway, add the rest of the spring onions, or continue testing every 15 seconds until it does (you won't be testing for long!). Fry for 90 seconds until the oil is bright green and the spring onions are just beginning to colour. Use a slotted spoon or strainer to lift the spring onions out of the oil onto the kitchen paper. Turn the heat off under the oil and immediately add the black onion seeds.

Variations
Replace the beetroot with carrots, prepared and cooked in the same way. The mint can be swapped for parsley, chervil or dill.

Stir the rest of the mint and the lemon juice into the pasta, then use tongs to lift the pasta into warm bowls. Crumble over the cheese, then sprinkle over the fried spring onions and spoon over a generous amount of the green onion oil. Any extra oil can be drizzled over fried or poached eggs, or hummus for a savoury kick.

Cheesy Curried Root Vegetable Pasties

The first time I made these sunny spiced pasties, they were demolished, so be assured that the piquancy isn't too hot. I like to use all-butter shortcrust pastry, which is typically found in the chilled aisle near the butter. The filling for these pasties makes more than you need, but it will keep covered in the fridge for up to 5 days and can be used to fill more pasties, or served warm alongside rice or naan breads with mango chutney.

TIMINGS: 1¾ HOURS
MAKES 8 PASTIES

1 small swede (rutabaga)
(about 450g/1lb)
200g (7oz) sweet potato
200g (7oz) Jerusalem artichokes
(sunchokes)
2 onions, roughly sliced into wedges
2 tbsp coconut oil, melted
1 tbsp medium curry powder
1 tsp black mustard seeds
25ml (1oz/1½ tbsp) freshly squeezed
lime juice
1 x 400g (14oz) can chickpeas,
drained
Bunch of coriander (cilantro), leaves
and tender stalks roughly chopped
225g (8oz) extra mature Cheddar
cheese, grated
2 x 375g (13oz) ready-rolled sheets
of all-butter shortcrust pastry
1 egg, beaten
1 tsp cumin seeds
Salt

To serve
Mango chutney
Quick Vegetable Pickles
(see page 178)

Preheat the oven to 200°C/400°F/Gas 6.

Peel the swede, sweet potato and Jerusalem artichokes and cut into rough 1.5cm (⅝in) cubes. Tip them into a large roasting tin and stir in the onions, coconut oil, curry powder, mustard seeds and 2 teaspoons of salt. Roast the vegetables for 25–30 minutes, shaking the roasting tin a couple of times during this time. Remove from the oven when the vegetables are tender to the point of a sharp knife, leaving the oven on. Set aside and allow to cool before mixing in the lime juice, chickpeas, coriander and Cheddar. Taste the mixture and adjust the seasoning. Lay a sheet of baking parchment over the roasting tin to cook the pasties.

Working with one sheet at a time, unroll the pastry and use a rolling pin to roll it out gently to roughly 45cm x 30cm (17¾ x 12in). Cut as many 18cm (7in) circles as you can from the pastry, before gathering the excess and rolling it out again to cut out more pastry circles. You're aiming for 8 x 18cm (3¼ x 7in) pastry circles to form the pasties.

Place the bowl of beaten egg on the worktop, along with a small bowl of water to help with sealing. Dip a clean finger in the water bowl and run it around the circumference of one of the pastry circles. Use a dessertspoon to place 2 heaped spoonfuls of the curried vegetable filling into the centre of the pastry. Lift half the pastry over the filling to meet the opposite side of the circle and press down to seal. Either fold and crimp the sealed side, or use a fork to press down along it. The filled pasties can be frozen at this stage for up to 3 months.

Brush the pastry with beaten egg, sprinkle with cumin seeds and transfer to the prepared roasting tin. Repeat with the remaining pastry and filling.

Bake the pasties in the oven for 10 minutes, before turning the temperature down to 180°C/350°F/Gas 4 to cook for a further 25 minutes. If you're cooking the pasties from frozen, brush the pastry with beaten egg and allow for an extra 10 minutes at 180°C/350°F/Gas 4. Check that the pasties are piping hot in the centre before eating.

Serve with mango chutney and Quick Vegetable Pickles.

Variations
Replace one of the onions with a small bulb of fennel. Replace the swede with the same weight of cauliflower, cut into bite-sized florets.

Shaved Celeriac & Hazelnut Caesar

You know a recipe is a banger when you make it three times in a week, as I did with this Caesar. The celeriac slicing is easiest with a mandoline, which is a very useful kitchen tool for vegetable cookery. You could also peel the celeriac into the bowl with a potato peeler, but this is a much lengthier process and tough on your hands, so be forewarned... The celeriac gets tossed in the light Caesar dressing before the salad is served, which helps to soften and flavour every slice.

TIMINGS: 30 MINUTES
SERVES 6 AS A STARTER OR SIDE

For the salad
150g (5½oz) sourdough bread
2 tbsp light olive oil
50g (1¾oz) hazelnuts
1 small celeriac (celery root)
    (about 500g/1lb 2oz), peeled
½ lemon
1 small head radicchio
    (about 150g/5½oz)
10 red grapes
20g (⅔oz) Parmesan cheese
Salt and pepper

For the Caesar dressing
2 garlic cloves
1 tbsp drained capers in brine
4 tbsp tahini
1 heaped tsp Dijon mustard
40ml (1½fl oz/2½ tbsp) lemon juice
2 tbsp extra virgin olive oil
30g (1oz) Parmesan cheese,
    finely grated

Preheat the oven to 200°C/400°F/Gas 6.

Tear the bread into bite-sized chunks, arrange on a baking tray so that there's no overlap and drizzle over the oil. Season with salt and pepper, then toss to distribute the oil evenly among the bread pieces. Place on the middle shelf in the oven to crisp for 12–15 minutes, shaking once or twice. Spread the hazelnuts on a separate, small baking tray and place on the bottom shelf in the oven to toast for 10–12 minutes until deep golden and fragrant, turning once. Remove both trays from the oven and tip the hazelnuts into the centre of a clean tea towel. Wrap them up to trap the heat, and set aside.

Meanwhile, make the Caesar dressing. Chop the garlic and capers together on a board very finely, almost to a paste, then scrape into a large mixing bowl. I say large, because you'll be using this bowl for the vegetables, too. Add the remaining dressing ingredients and whisk together with 5 tablespoons of water, added 1 tablespoon at a time, until the dressing is the thickness of cream and tastes deeply savoury. Season generously with black pepper. Spoon one-third of the dressing into a small bowl or jug and set aside.

Use the thinnest setting on the mandoline to shave the celeriac into the bowl with the dressing. Squeeze over a few drops of lemon juice as you go to prevent the celeriac from turning brown. Once all the celeriac is in the bowl with the majority of the dressing, use clean hands to toss both together. Rub the hazelnuts in the tea towel to loosen their papery skins, then lift the nuts onto a board, discarding the skins, and roughly chop.

To assemble the salad, separate the leaves of the radicchio and discard the core. Layer the dressed celeriac with the radicchio (I like to keep these undressed initially, because the magenta of the leaves is quite striking), sourdough croutons and hazelnuts. Finely slice the grapes into thin rounds and arrange over the top of the salad. Finely grate over the 20g (⅔oz) cheese and serve with the reserved dressing for drizzling over.

Variations
This can be made with the same weight of Jerusalem artichokes, kohlrabi or oca (a mild tuber) for a different flavour.

Jewelled Stovetop Rice

For a dish that looks so classy, and tastes complex, it's hard to believe that everything happens in one pan. Fresh curry leaves have a distinctive flavour that's hard to define, but I'll try: notes of clove, citrus and a characteristic savouriness are released when they're fried in oil. I buy mine from an Indian supermarket, and the leaves I don't use straightaway can be frozen in a sealed bag for up to a year. If you can't find them, leave them out (the dried ones don't carry the same potency), but they do add a certain flair, so they're worth tracking down if you can.

TIMINGS: 40 MINUTES
SERVES 4

200g (7oz/generous 1 cup) basmati rice
1 tbsp butter
2 tbsp rapeseed (canola) oil
2 onions, finely sliced
500g (1lb 2oz) golden beetroot, peeled and cut into 1cm (½in) cubes
150ml (5fl oz/scant ⅔ cup) white wine
50g (1¾oz) cashews, roughly chopped
2 green chillies, finely chopped
6cm (2½in) piece fresh ginger, grated
2 garlic cloves, finely chopped
2 bay leaves
40 curry leaves
1 tsp cumin seeds
1 tsp black mustard seeds

Pared peel of 1 unwaxed lime
400ml (14fl oz/1¾ cups) vegetable stock
Salt and pepper

To serve
1 small chioggia beetroot, finely sliced on a mandoline
Juice of 1 lime
3 tbsp pomegranate seeds
½ small bunch of coriander (cilantro), leaves and tender stems roughly chopped
Greek yoghurt

Place the basmati rice in a sieve and rinse under a running tap, agitating the rice grains with your hands to rinse away as much starch as possible. When the water that runs through the sieve into the sink is no longer cloudy, tip the rice into a bowl and cover with 2cm (¾in) fresh water. Set aside.

Heat the butter and oil in a large, deep frying pan over a medium heat. When the butter is melted and bubbling noisily, add the onions to the pan along with a pinch of salt and generous grind of black pepper. Cook, stirring regularly, until the onions are soft and well on their way to being caramelised, about 12–15 minutes. Turn the heat under the pan up to high, then stir in the beetroot, pour in the wine and cover the pan with a lid. Cook, without peeking, for 8 minutes, then remove the lid and check the tenderness of the beetroot with a sharp knife. If it still feels hard, continue to cook for a few minutes with the lid on (adding a splash of water if all of the wine has evaporated). Once tender, turn the heat down to medium again and stir through the cashews, chillies, ginger, garlic, bay leaves and curry leaves. Cook for a minute until fragrant, then add the dried spices. Drain the rice, then stir it through the spiced vegetable mixture, along with the lime peel. Pour over the vegetable stock, cover the pan with a lid and cook for 8 minutes.

Meanwhile, toss the sliced chioggia beetroot in the lime juice in a small bowl and set aside.

Remove the pan from the heat and leave it with the lid on, without peeking, for 8 minutes before serving. This will help a crispy rice base to form.

Serve the rice in the pan at the table with the pomegranate seeds and coriander sprinkled over the top. Arrange the stripy beetroot slices in the middle of the rice and serve immediately with a dollop of Greek yoghurt on the side.

Variations
Replace the golden beetroot with cubes of celeriac (celery root), which will need a few minutes less to cook through until tender.

Savoury Root Vegetable Crumble

There's something truly pleasing about a savoury crumble because a) it's a playful twist on a typical Sunday roast dessert, and b) it's basically a low-effort super crispy pie. I use a mixture of sweet and more bitter root vegetables for maximum flavour, but you can certainly play around with the quantities to make it work with what you have in.

TIMINGS: 1 HOUR
SERVES 4–6

350g (12oz) celeriac (celery root)
350g (12oz) swede (rutabaga)
200g (7oz) carrots
2 red onions, cut into 8 wedges
50ml (1¾oz/3½ tbsp) freshly squeezed lemon juice (about 1–2 lemons)
Olive oil, for roasting
25 green olives, pitted, roughly chopped
1 x 700g (1lb 9oz) jar white beans, such as cannellini or butter beans, drained and rinsed (or 2 x 400g/14oz cans)
Small bunch of tarragon, leaves picked
Salt and pepper

For the sauce
50g (1¾oz/3½ tbsp) unsalted butter
50g (1¾oz/6 tbsp) plain white (all-purpose) flour
550ml (19fl oz/scant 2½ cups) whole milk
1 tbsp Dijon mustard

50g (1¾oz) extra mature Cheddar cheese, grated
40g (1½oz) Parmesan cheese, grated
¼ whole nutmeg, grated

For the crumble topping
50g (1¾oz/3½ tbsp) unsalted butter
150g (5½oz) breadcrumbs
50g (1¾oz) hazelnuts, roughly chopped
100g (3½oz) smoked hard cheese, grated
50g (1¾oz/½ cup) jumbo oats

To serve
Wilted greens, sauerkraut or pickled vegetables (see page 178)

Peel and cut the celeriac, swede and carrots into rough 2cm (¾in) pieces. Arrange the root vegetables and onions in a 20 x 30cm (8 x 12in) roasting dish. Pour over the lemon juice, drizzle over enough olive oil to coat and season with salt and pepper. Stir to combine, then cover the dish tightly with foil and roast in the oven for 20 minutes, until the vegetables are tender.

Meanwhile, make the cheesy sauce. Melt the butter in a small saucepan over a medium heat and stir in the flour. Stir constantly for 2 minutes, until the mixture begins to smell toasty and has turned a shade or two darker. Slowly pour in the milk and whisk enthusiastically to prevent any lumps from forming. Turn the heat down to low and continue to stir regularly for 12–15 minutes, until the sauce thickens to coat the back of a wooden spoon. Remove from the heat and add the mustard, both cheeses and the nutmeg. Season generously with salt and pepper.

For the crumble topping, rub the butter into the breadcrumbs, then stir through the remaining ingredients.

Remove the vegetables from the oven, lift away the foil and stir through the olives, beans and tarragon. Pour over the white sauce and stir to coat every vegetable, bean and olive with the cheesy sauce. Scatter over the crumble topping, then return to the oven to bake for 25 minutes, until the top is golden and crisp and the sauce is visibly bubbling at the sides.

Allow to cool in the dish for 5 minutes before spooning onto warm plates to serve with wilted greens, sauerkraut or pickled vegetables.

Variations
Replace the celeriac or swede with potatoes.

6

TOMATOES

&

PEPPERS

For simplicity's sake (as well as my personal preference), I'm focusing on the traffic-light-red end of the spectrum for the stars of this chapter. Every week, most of us will be cooking with a tomato or pepper in one form or another — sliced, tinned, puréed, in a salad, in hot sauce or harissas — these glossy, sweet, sun-soaked vegetables (botanically fruits, really) add pep to our dinners throughout the year.

Look for fruits that have a smooth and shiny skin; any wrinkling is a sign of moisture (and sugar) loss, resulting in a dull flavour.

Tomatoes I struggle to think of a fruit or vegetable that's more industrially preserved than the tomato — we probably have Heinz to thank for that. While I love tomato ketchup as much as the next person, in my kitchen it's always juicy chopped cherry or vine tomatoes, purée or passata that I weave into our dinners a few times each week. If you're cooking with fresh tomatoes, my advice would be to always have a little taste before you start — in fact, this is my motto for life. Any that aren't bright can be livened up by chopping roughly and tossing with a splash of red wine vinegar and a pinch of salt and sugar — this is a method which works well for salsas and tomato salads, too.

I know we live in a global economy, where we can get any fruit or vegetable no matter the season, but fresh tomatoes do tend to be better in every way in the summer months. If the days are short and cold, I'd open a can of juicy chopped tomatoes to brighten up a dish.

Peppers Crunchy red peppers are the ripest of them all — green peppers are just cousins of the red ones that have been picked before they've ripened and had a chance to turn plump and sweet. I prefer a cooked pepper myself, and to speed things up I'll often use a jarred pepper that has been packed after roasting. To cook peppers yourself (for example for the romesco on page 33, or the rigatoni on page 128), either cook whole over a gas flame, turning often for 15 minutes, until the skins are completely charred, or roast on a baking parchment-lined baking sheet in an oven heated to 200°C/400°F/Gas 6 until the peppers are completely soft and the skin charred and wrinkled. Tip the peppers into a bowl and cover with a plate (the steam will help to loosen the skins). Once cool, peel away the skins and discard with the stalk and seeds before adding to your dishes.

Grilled Summer Vegetables with Crispy Fried Feta & Honey

A few years ago, I was lucky to work with one of my vegetable heroines, Anna Jones, who introduced me to blistered feta, wobbly and wonderful hot from the oven. I take it one step further, wrapping it in filo pastry to create a brittle shell that turns golden as the feta fries. Be sure to remove the feta from the fridge a couple of hours before cooking, so that it comes up to room temperature, otherwise the feta might stay cold in the middle.

TIMINGS: 45 MINUTES
SERVES 2

For the vegetables
4 tbsp extra virgin olive oil
20 basil leaves
1 tbsp red wine vinegar
1 garlic clove, crushed
3 (bell) peppers (red, yellow
    or orange)
2 courgettes (zucchini)
200g (7oz) cherry tomatoes
Salt and pepper

For the crispy fried feta
4 tbsp runny honey
1 red chilli, deseeded and
    finely chopped
1 sprig thyme
4 sheets filo (phyllo) pastry
Extra virgin olive oil, for brushing
    and frying
200g (7oz) block feta, at room
    temperature

Preheat a griddle pan on the highest heat on the hob.

Combine the oil, basil, vinegar and garlic in a large mixing bowl (you'll need the bowl to be large enough to hold all of the cooked vegetables), season generously with salt and pepper and stir to combine.

Cut the peppers into chunky strips, discarding the seeds and stalk. Without any overlap, griddle them for 8–10 minutes on each side, until the skin begins to wrinkle and they turn soft and smoky. When the peppers are cooked, stir them through the oil mixture and cover the bowl with a plate to trap the steam. Next, slice the courgettes into ½cm (¼in) thick lengths, then griddle them for 3–4 minutes each side, until softened and striped. Add the courgettes to the bowl with the peppers and stir to coat in the marinade. Cover the bowl again with a plate. Finally, char the cherry tomatoes on the griddle for a few minutes until the skins are cracked and blistered. Stir through with the other vegetables and marinade and cover the bowl with the plate again. Set aside while you cook the feta.

Pour the honey into a small saucepan (a lightly oiled measuring spoon will help the honey to slip off without any stickiness) and add the chilli and thyme. Heat until the honey starts to bubble, then remove from the heat. The longer you leave the honey to steep, the spicier it will be.

Brush two sheets of the filo with olive oil all over, then stack one on top of the other. Place the room temperature feta in the centre of the sheets and pull in the corners of the pastry to cover the feta and wrap it up like a present. Flip the feta over so that the folded corners are on the bottom. Repeat the oiling and wrapping with the remaining sheets, ensuring the folded corners are on the other side so that the filo wrapper is of an even thickness.

Heat enough olive oil to cover the base of a small frying pan. Carefully lower the filo-wrapped feta, seam side down, into the pan and fry for 3–4 minutes, using a spoon to splash the sides with oil to help them crisp and brown evenly. Use a slotted spatula to flip the feta to fry on the other side for another 3–4 minutes.

While the feta is frying on the second side, tip the vegetables onto a serving platter, along with all of the marinade. Lift the cooked feta onto the vegetables using the slotted spatula and pour over the hot honey just before serving.

Any leftover vegetables can be kept covered in the fridge for up to 3 days.

Variations
You could char other summer vegetables to add to the mix, such as aubergines (eggplants), spring onions (scallions) or green beans.

Easy Black Bean Quesadillas with Tomato & Pomegranate Salsa

Smoky, cheesy, just-right-spicy quesadillas and a bright, tangy salsa – this just needs a salty-rimmed margarita to make you feel like you're on holiday.

You're going to use the same frying pan to cook each hot element of this recipe to save on washing up, so even though your pan might feel on the larger side to cook the red onions, use one that can easily hold the tortillas, with ample room for flipping.

TIMINGS: 30 MINUTES
SERVES 4

For the salsa
250g (9oz) cherry tomatoes, quartered
¼ large red onion, very finely chopped
1 green chilli, deseeded and finely chopped
125g (4½oz) pomegranate seeds
¼ cucumber, roughly chopped
2 tbsp extra virgin olive oil
Leaves from 1 small bunch of coriander (cilantro)

For the quesadillas
1 tbsp coconut oil, plus extra, for frying
1 tbsp tomato purée (paste)
¾ large red onion, roughly chopped
2 garlic cloves, crushed
1 tsp ground cumin
2 tsp chipotle paste
1 tsp dried oregano
1 x 400g (14oz) can black beans, drained
125g (4½oz) ball of Mozzarella cheese, grated
100g (3½oz) mature Cheddar cheese, grated
30ml (1fl oz/2 tbsp) freshly squeezed lime juice (1–2 limes)
8 tortillas
Salt and pepper

Toss together the tomatoes, red onion and green chilli for the salsa in a mixing bowl with ½ teaspoon salt. Cover and set aside.

For the quesadilla filling, heat the coconut oil in a large frying pan. Add the tomato purée and red onion to the pan, along with a pinch of salt. Fry, stirring occasionally, for 8 minutes until the onions are soft and translucent and the tomato purée has turned from bright red to brick red. Stir in the garlic, cumin and chipotle paste and cook for a minute more. Remove from the heat and stir in the oregano before scraping everything into a medium mixing bowl. Add the beans, both cheeses and lime juice to the bowl, then season with salt and pepper and taste the bean mixture. When you're happy, roughly mash with a potato masher to break up the beans. Wipe out the frying pan with a piece of kitchen paper (there's no need to wash it up), then return to the hob.

To construct the quesadillas, add a teaspoon of coconut oil to the frying pan and melt over a medium heat. Place a tortilla in the centre, then spoon in 2 heaped dessertspoons of the black bean mixture to the middle. Use the back of the spoon to roughly spread the mixture over the surface of the flatbread. Place another tortilla over the top of the bean mixture and press down with the back of a spatula. Cook for 3–4 minutes, until the cheese begins to melt and the bottom tortilla is crisp and golden. Flip and cook on the other side for another 3–4 minutes. Repeat with the remaining tortillas and bean mixture, adding a little more oil to the pan each time it looks dry. Keep the cooked quesadillas warm in a low (150°C/300°F/Gas 2) oven on a large tray while you cook the rest.

To finish the salsa, add the pomegranate, cucumber and oil to the bowl with the tomatoes and stir to combine. Roughly chop three-quarters of the coriander and stir through the salsa mixture.

Cut the quesadillas into four triangular wedges and serve on a board, sprinkled with the reserved coriander. Spoon the salsa over the quesadillas before eating with hands, a few napkins, and margaritas or chilled beer.

20-Minute Tomato & Butterbean Traybake

Unfortunately for recipe writers like me, grills are the enemy of consistency. I've made a few suggestions to guarantee cooked and perfectly blistered vegetables for this dish, including the tray you use to cook everything in. Using one with a bit of depth will encourage the vegetables to steam as they char under the heat of the grill, making sure they soften and cook right through.

TIMINGS: 20 MINUTES
SERVES 4

2 tbsp light olive oil, plus extra for greasing
1 red onion, cut into 10 wedges
1 fennel bulb, cut lengthways into 1cm (½in) slices
2 tbsp red wine vinegar
1 x 600g (1lb 5oz) jar butterbeans, drained
1 tbsp rose harissa paste
300g (10½oz) cherry tomatoes, halved
20 black olives, such as Kalamata, pitted
150g (5½oz) ball of Mozzarella cheese, torn in bite-sized chunks
1 x quantity Garlicky Vinaigrette (see page 179)
Leaves from ½ small bunch of oregano
Leaves from ½ small bunch of basil
Salt and pepper
Crusty bread, to serve (optional)

Preheat the grill (broiler) to high.

Lightly grease a deep 30 x 40cm (12 x 16in) roasting dish with oil and, in it, toss the red onion and fennel with enough oil to coat, as well as the red wine vinegar. Season with salt and pepper. Place the dish under the grill for 7 minutes, shaking once halfway through.

While the fennel and onion are under the grill, tip the beans onto a piece of kitchen paper and pat dry with another piece of paper, or a clean tea towel. Scrape the beans into a mixing bowl and toss with the rose harissa.

Remove the tray from under the grill and add the harissa-beans, tomatoes and olives to the tray. Place under the grill for another 12 minutes, removing every 2–3 minutes to turn all of the vegetables over with a spatula. Depending on the ferocity of your grill, this may take a few minutes more or less until the vegetables are tender throughout and charring in places.

Remove the tray from the grill, scatter over the Mozzarella and return the tray to under the grill for a minute until the cheese is melted and bubbling.

Use a spatula to turn everything in the tray onto a serving platter and drizzle over the dressing. Scatter the herb leaves over the top and season with salt and pepper before serving while everything is still piping hot, with crusty bread, if preferred.

Variations
Replace half the weight of tomatoes with 1 red (bell) pepper, finely sliced into 1cm (½in) strips.

One Pan Pepper & Black Olive Rigatoni

The rigatoni (you could use other tubular shapes instead) releases its starch as it cooks, self-saucing with the umami ingredients. I've made this again and again when time is short and I want to get a mid-week meal on the table quickly. If you have plenty of time and feel for using fresh peppers, you can use two large red peppers, roasted until soft (see page 120). The optional ricotta adds a mild, creamy accent to the rich sauce if that's what you're in the mood for.

TIMINGS: 30 MINUTES
SERVES 4 GENEROUSLY

80ml (2½fl oz/5 tbsp) extra virgin olive oil
4 tbsp tomato purée (paste)
4 garlic cloves, finely sliced
50g (1¾oz) flaked (sliced) almonds
500g (1lb 2oz) dried rigatoni
2 large red (bell) peppers from the jar, thinly sliced
20g (⅔oz) black olives in brine, pitted and roughly chopped
Pinch of dried chilli flakes
Small bunch of basil
1.25 litres (44fl oz/5½ cups) vegetable stock
Juice and zest of 1 lemon
Salt and pepper
100g (3½oz) ricotta cheese, to serve (optional)

Pour the oil into a wide, shallow pan for which you have a lid. Measure the tomato purée in too, then cook over a medium heat, stirring regularly, for 5 minutes, until the oil is bright red and the tomato purée is a much darker, brick red shade. Stir in the garlic and almonds and cook for a couple more minutes until golden and fragrant. At this stage, the tomato purée in the mixture can start to look quite dark, but it can go almost to black before it turns bitter and burns, so keep everything moving and manage the heat to ensure a rich, savoury flavour develops without anything catching.

Stir in the rigatoni, peppers, olives, 2 tablespoons of brine from the olive jar and the chilli flakes. Roughly chop the leaves and tender stems of half the bunch of basil, setting the rest aside for later. Stir the basil through the pasta until everything is evenly combined, then pour over the vegetable stock and bring the mixture to the boil. Cover the pan with a lid and boil for 15 minutes, removing the lid every 90 seconds to stir the pasta and prevent it from sticking.

When nearly all the liquid has been absorbed, remove the pan from the heat and zest over the lemon. Cut the lemon in half and squeeze over the juice. Spoon the rigatoni into warm bowls and top with the remaining basil leaves, and the ricotta, broken up with a spoon over each portion, if using.

Tomato, Ginger & Coconut Soup

Tomato and coconut is a seriously underrated flavour pairing. The acidity from the tomatoes is a sharp foil to the sweet fattiness of coconut. I suppose it's a modern twist on cream of tomato soup, with an added boost of protein from the beans. The spiced oil that gets drizzled on top of the deceptively rich soup adds a welcome hint of crunch and pops of earthy spice.

TIMINGS: 30 MINUTES
SERVES 4

2 tbsp coconut oil
2 onions, finely sliced
2 tbsp tomato purée (paste)
12cm (4½in) piece of ginger
2 garlic cloves
1 tsp ground cumin
400g (14oz) can peeled tomatoes
400g can (14oz) cannellini beans, drained
400g can (14oz) full-fat coconut milk
Salt

For the spiced oil
2 tbsp coconut oil
4 stalks of curry leaves, leaves picked
½ tsp black mustard seeds

Melt the coconut oil in a large saucepan. Add the onions, ½ teaspoon of salt and the tomato purée to the pan. Stir to combine, then cook for 10–12 minutes until the tomato purée has turned a deep rusty colour and the onions are sweet and tender. Add a splash of water to the pan from time to time if the mixture looks as though it's beginning to stick and burn. A word of warning: tomato purée can taste metallic and end up overpowering other ingredients if not cooked through properly. It's for this reason that I always try to fry it a bit first.

Cut 4cm (1½in) off the ginger, then peel this smaller piece and roughly grate it, along with the garlic. Add the ginger, garlic and cumin to the pan and stir for 1–2 minutes until fragrant. Tip in the tomatoes and break them up with a wooden spoon. Bring to a simmer and allow the tomatoes to cook for 5 minutes, stirring occasionally, before adding the beans and coconut milk. Fill one of the cans with water and tip into the pan with the other ingredients. Simmer for 15 minutes, then remove from the heat.

Use a stick blender to blend until smooth, then sieve the soup to make it as smooth as possible. This step is worth following – it doesn't take a minute as the soup is already fairly smooth and it does make for a more pure, pleasing texture.

Grate the remaining ginger (there's no need to peel this piece), then hold it over the soup in a fist and squeeze the ginger juice into the soup. Discard the ginger pulp. Stir to combine, then taste the soup and add more salt if needed.

Heat the remaining coconut oil in a small frying pan. When it's melted and beginning to form ripples in the pan, add the curry leaves and mustard seeds and fry for 45 seconds until the curry leaves curl and crisp and the seeds begin to pop. Ladle the soup into warm bowls, and spoon the hot oil and aromatics over the soup. Serve immediately. Any extra soup can be chilled for up to a week, or frozen in a sealed container for up to 3 months before being defrosted and warmed through.

Variations
You can use 4 shallots instead of the onions (they will need half the cooking time). Instead of cannellini beans, use a can of butter beans if that's what you have instead.

Fresh Cheesy Corn Polenta with the World's Best Tinned Tomato Sauce

Something magical happens when pine nuts are pounded into a rich, buttery paste and folded through molten tomato sauce; the bright red sauce becomes deeply savoury, rather than pleasantly sharp–sweet. I deploy it in pasta; as a pizza topping; or simmered for an extra 10 minutes into a dip, drizzled with tahini. Alongside the corn polenta, though, it's really special; somehow the sweet contrast of the rich corn polenta makes the sauce taste more vibrant.

TIMINGS: 45 MINUTES
SERVES 4

For the polenta
6 ears of corn
25g (1oz/1½ tbsp) unsalted butter
2 tbsp extra virgin olive oil
4 shallots, finely sliced
400ml (14fl oz/1¾ cups) weak
    vegetable stock
100g (3½oz) soft goats' cheese
100g (3½oz) extra mature Cheddar
    cheese
Salt and pepper

For the tomato sauce
2 tbsp extra virgin olive oil
2 garlic cloves, finely sliced
2 bay leaves
1 x 400g (14oz) can chopped
    tomatoes
50g (1¾oz) pine nuts, toasted

To serve
Grilled broccoli (see page 22)
1 x quantity Bashed Walnut & Shallot
    Relish (see page 184)

Variations
Serve the Grilled Summer Vegetables (see page 121) on top of the corn polenta instead.

Remove the papery husks and stringy silks from the corn. Stand one of them upright in a bowl with the pointy end toward the ceiling and use a sharp knife to slice down the length, turning the corn as you go, until every kernel is in the bowl. Repeat with the remaining corn, until they're all stripped of the yolk-yellow kernels. Discard the corn centres (or save them for stock).

Heat the butter and oil in a large saucepan over a medium–high heat. Once all the butter is melted and sizzling, add the shallots and season generously with salt and black pepper. Cook, stirring occasionally, for 6–8 minutes, until the shallots are completely soft and translucent and beginning to colour. Add the corn and the stock and bring to the boil, then turn the heat down to a simmer and cook for 8 minutes. Use a slotted spoon to lift three-quarters of the corn into the bowl of a food processor, leaving the liquid and remaining one-quarter of the corn mixture in the pan. Blitz the corn in the processor until smooth, then return it to the pan over a low heat and stir in the cheeses. Taste and adjust the seasoning, then keep warm on the lowest heat while you make the tomato sauce, stirring occasionally to prevent anything sticking to the base of the pan.

To make the tomato sauce, heat the oil in a small saucepan over a medium heat. Add the garlic and stir continuously for 30–45 seconds until the garlic is just beginning to turn golden. Stir in the bay leaves and the chopped tomatoes, then season with salt and stir to combine. Bring to a gentle simmer. Use a pestle and mortar to crush the pine nuts until a smooth nut butter forms, then stir the pine nut butter through the tomato sauce. Simmer for 15 minutes, then taste and adjust the seasoning.

To serve, spoon the sweetcorn mixture into shallow warm bowls and top with the tomato sauce, broccoli and a spoonful of Bashed Walnut & Shallot Relish.

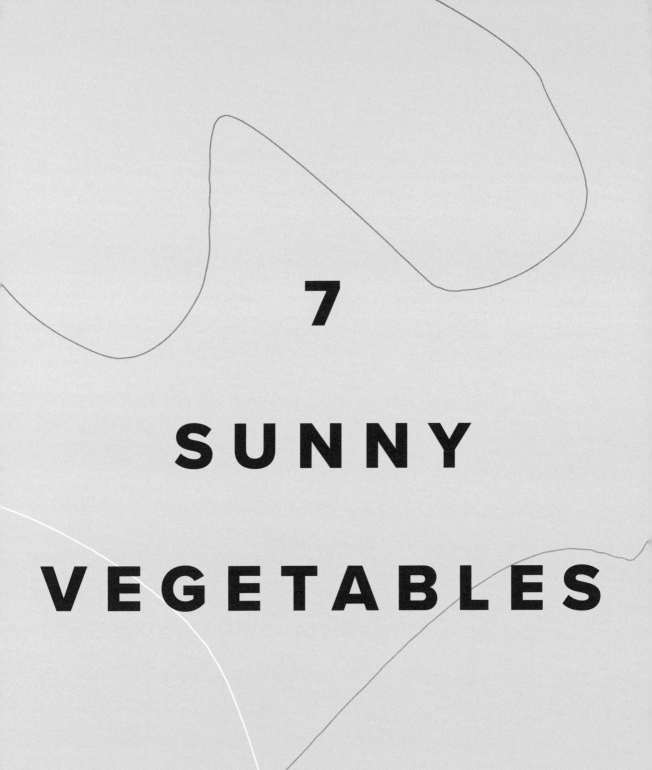

7

SUNNY

VEGETABLES

The sunshine, beta carotene pigment is common in all of the vegetables in this chapter. The rich, yolky hue found in carrots, sweet potatoes and squash is converted to vitamin A in the body, which anecdotally is said to promote physical and mental health in myriad ways. The other characteristic shared by the edible stars of the following pages is their bright sweetness, which in carrots is amplified by frosts when they're in the ground (the frost stress dials up their natural sugars, which caramelise in the pan). Generally, squash and sweet potatoes cook in a similar way, whereas carrots are denser, so the thicker ones will take longer to become tender.

Carrots Fresh, young carrots are sold with their edible leaves attached, which resemble the flavour of grassy fresh parsley (although they're tough, so best steamed or blanched before being added to dishes or whizzed into pesto). The leaves should be separated from the roots as soon as you get home to prevent the pointy young roots from turning floppy. Young carrots just need a scrub (there's no need to peel them) before cooking, slicing or grating into salads. Like other roots, carrots can be stored for up to 6 months after harvesting given the right conditions (dark, cool, well-ventilated). Carrots sold without their leaves attached are still sweet, but less delicate tasting, so benefit from being paired with bold flavours.

Winter Squash Traffic-light-orange Butternut, Crown Prince, Acorn, etc. – these are all technically fruits from the cucurbit family (see also courgettes (zucchini) and cucumbers). Pumpkin is also in this family, and like pumpkin, each squash's seeds can be roasted to be eaten if you have the time to rinse and roast them. I like the natural sweetness of squash with peanuts, coconut and lime when my palate is jaded and craving sunshine, or stirred through with butter and topped with brittle fried sage leaves and crunchy golden hazelnuts in a risotto or pasta for the ultimate comfort food.

Sweet Potatoes Yes, they can be cooked into chips or jackets, but sweet potatoes are more tender and (obviously) sweeter than their white-fleshed friends. I prefer not to treat a sweet potato as a *potato*, but like an entirely different vegetable. Its sweetness and creamy flesh means that it behaves more like the other vegetables in this chapter, and pairs well with similar ingredients (sweet potato and peanut soup, sharpened with lime, is a revelation). They work well with spice (try them in the Spiced Root Vegetable & Lime Pancakes on page 99) and are great contrasted with salty ingredients like halloumi, olives and capers, too.

Ricotta & Nutmeg Dumplings with Whipped Squash & Crispy Sage

TIMINGS: 1½ HOURS,
PLUS RESTING TIME
SERVES 4 AS A MAIN,
OR 6 AS A STARTER

For the dumplings

500g (1lb 2oz) ricotta
75g (2½oz/½ cup plus 1 tbsp) Italian
    00 flour
50g (1¾oz) Parmesan cheese, finely
    grated, plus extra to serve
1 egg
½ whole nutmeg, grated

For the whipped squash and crispy sage

1 x 1kg (2lb 4oz) butternut squash
1 garlic bulb
4 tbsp Greek yoghurt
1 tsp Dijon mustard
Pinch of dried chilli flakes
50ml (1¾fl oz/3½ tbsp) extra virgin
    olive oil
50g (1¾oz/3½ tbsp) unsalted butter
Leaves from a small bunch of sage
    (about 50), picked and stalks
    discarded
Salt and black pepper

The fried sage adds a welcome contrast to the rich creaminess of the sauce and dumplings. A couple of handfuls of sage leaves will do the trick, and so long as they don't overlap too much in the pan (which inhibits frying and crisping), you'll end up with a brittle herby garnish that you'll want to sprinkle over everything.

Preheat the oven to 200°C/400°F/Gas 6.

Lay four sheets of kitchen paper on a board, stacked on top of each other. Peel away the film from the ricotta container and pour away any excess liquid that's pooling around the cheese. Tip the ricotta into the centre of the kitchen paper and cover with another four sheets of kitchen paper. Place another board on top and weigh down with a heavy jar or bowl. Set aside for 15 minutes to drain.

Meanwhile, halve the squash lengthways and remove the seeds. Arrange the squash on a roasting tray, with the cut-sides facing up. Slice away the pointy, papery top of the garlic bulb, so that the top of each clove is visible. Drizzle the squash and garlic with enough olive oil to coat, rubbing the oil all over as you go, and sprinkle over a pinch of salt and a generous few grinds of black pepper. Place the tray on the middle shelf in the oven to cook for 45 minutes, until the squash is tender throughout to the point of a sharp knife. Check it after 30 minutes or so as the cooking time can vary depending on the age and density of the squash.

While the squash is in the oven, pull away the kitchen paper on the ricotta (it should lift away without sticking) and scrape the cheese into a medium mixing bowl. Add the remaining ingredients for the dumplings to the bowl and season well with salt and pepper. Use a spatula to mix the ricotta with the other ingredients, and as soon as it comes together in a ball, stop mixing – this should take no longer than 20 turns of the spatula. This is to ensure the flour isn't over-worked, making the dumplings ultimately tough, as a perfect dumpling relies on its cloud-like nature. Transfer to the fridge to chill for 30 minutes while the squash continues to roast.

Once the squash is cooked, remove from the oven and, when it's cool enough to handle, peel away the skin (or if it's very tough, use a spoon to scoop the flesh out of the skin) and transfer the flesh to the bowl of a food processor. Squeeze the garlic cloves out of the bulb into the food processor by pressing up from the base of the bulb, as though it's a tube of toothpaste. Add the yoghurt, mustard and chilli flakes too, then cover the processor with a lid and, with the motor running, slowly pour in the olive oil in a steady stream. Season the whipped squash mixture with salt and pepper to taste. Transfer the squash mixture to a saucepan and keep warm over a low heat until you're ready to serve.

For the dumplings, bring a large pan of salted water to the boil. Place a sieve suspended over a bowl next to the hob. Use two teaspoons to shape the dumplings into little pointed rugby-ball shapes and drop them into the boiling water as you go. This will initially feel a little clunky, but you'll get into a rhythm. After you've dropped in six or so dumplings, they should start to bob to the surface after a minute. When they do, lift out with a slotted spoon and lower into the sieve. Even though they look delicate, they're pretty robust, so have faith. Repeat with the remaining mixture to cook around 30 dumplings.

Lay a couple of sheets of kitchen paper on a plate and place next to the hob. Melt the butter in a large frying pan over a medium–high heat. When it starts to bubble audibly, tip in the sage and use a slotted spatula to turn the leaves around in the butter until the butter stops sizzling and the sage leaves curl up. Use the spatula to lift the sage onto the kitchen paper to drain, leaving the butter in the pan. Gently tip the dumplings into the sage butter and warm through for a couple of minutes, shaking the pan a few times to turn the dumplings over without piercing them.

Spoon the squash mixture into warm bowls and top with 6–8 dumplings per person. Scatter a few sage leaves over the top and grate some extra Parmesan finely over each bowl.

The squash mixture can be made up to 5 days in advance and heated gently when everything else is ready to serve.

Variations
Roast other winter squash varieties (with the exception of spaghetti) in the same way. You may need to adjust the cooking time, depending on the age and size of the squash in question.

Speedy Spiced Carrot & Quinoa Fritters

When I want to get dinner on the table quickly, a meal cooked on the hob is usually my go-to, and these crispy fritters are rich in protein from the quinoa, and a great way to use up small amounts of carrots or a lone sweet potato.

A pouch of cooked quinoa speeds things along, but by all means cook your own if you have it, just be sure to drain and dry it well. The bright acidity of cherry tomatoes is the perfect complement to the crispy fritters, hot from the pan.

TIMINGS: 30 MINUTES
SERVES 4–6 (MAKES ABOUT 16)

For the tomatoes
200g (7oz) cherry tomatoes, quartered
1 small red onion, finely sliced
2 tsp red wine vinegar (optional)
Leaves from ¼ small bunch of mint, torn
2 tbsp extra virgin olive oil
Salt and pepper

For the fritters
2 carrots (about 250g/9oz), peeled and grated
Bunch of spring onions (scallions), white and light green parts finely sliced
100g (3½oz) feta, crumbled
1 x 250g (9oz) pouch cooked quinoa
1 red chilli, finely sliced
Leaves from ¾ small bunch of mint, roughly chopped
3 eggs, beaten
2 tbsp whole milk
3 tbsp plain white (all-purpose) flour
1 tsp baking powder
Neutral oil, such as light olive oil, for frying

Toss the cherry tomatoes with ¼ teaspoon salt, the red onion and red wine vinegar, then set aside while you make the fritters. This red wine vinegar and salt trick can revive even the most sad, flavourless tomatoes, but if yours are particularly bright and juicy, add the vinegar and salt to the onions and stir the cherry tomatoes through just before serving.

Toss the carrots, spring onions, feta, quinoa, chilli and mint together in a large mixing bowl. If you're using pre-cooked quinoa from a pouch, you may need to agitate the quinoa while the pouch is sealed to break up the seeds. (Fun fact! Quinoa is indeed a seed, not a grain, making it extra rich in protein.) Stir in the eggs, milk, flour and baking powder and season with salt and pepper (remembering the feta is salty).

Lay a couple of pieces of kitchen paper on top of a cooling rack by the hob. Heat enough oil to cover the base of a large frying pan by 1mm (⅟₃₂in) over a medium–high heat. A good measure of whether the oil is hot enough is if the mixture sizzles as soon as it hits the pan. When hot, add a teaspoon of the mixture and fry for a couple of minutes on each side to check the seasoning, adding more salt or pepper to the batter if you like. When you're happy, fry heaped dessertspoon-sized portions of the fritter mixture, three or four at a time, for 4 minutes on the first side, before flipping and cooking on the other side. Be sure to leave plenty of space between the fritters in the pan so that they turn crisp: if they're too closely packed together, they tend to steam instead and fall apart. Use a slotted spatula to transfer the cooked fritters to the prepared rack. Cook the remaining mixture in batches in the same way, adding more oil to the pan if it begins to look dry – don't be tempted to be too puritan about your cooking oil here, as too little can lead to the outside of the fritters burning before the inside is cooked. Fat is also a wonderful conductor of flavour.

Stir the mint and olive oil through the tomatoes. Serve a few fritters per person, along with some of the tomato salad on the side.

Variations
Use the same weight of grated sweet potato instead of the carrots.

Curried Butternut Squash & Fresh Herb Noodle Soup

I could eat this fresh and fragrant soup every day and not get bored. The ingredients are inspired by Malaysian and Singaporean *laksas,* which are usually lip-smackingly fishy, but I find the spicy coconut broth pairs perfectly with sweet squash. The aromatics and puffed tofu (which 'sucks up' the brothy sauce) can be found in Asian supermarkets or online.

TIMINGS: 1 HOUR
SERVES 4–6

For the curry paste
100g (3½oz) cashews
20g (⅔oz) coconut flakes
4 shallots, peeled and halved
2 red chillies, deseeded
2 green chillies, deseeded
6cm (2½in) piece galangal, peeled
6cm (2½in) piece ginger, peeled
4 garlic cloves
2 stalks lemongrass, roughly chopped
2 tsp tamarind paste
2 tsp ground cumin
2 tsp ground turmeric
1 tsp ground coriander
1 tsp soft brown sugar
1 tsp salt

For the soup
Vegetable oil, for frying
500g (1lb 2oz) butternut squash, peeled and cut into 2cm (¾in) cubes
1 x 400g (14oz) can coconut milk
800ml (28fl oz/3½ cups) vegetable stock
1 tbsp fish sauce, plus extra if needed
100g (3½oz) frozen peas
150g (5½oz) puffed tofu
Salt

To serve
300g (10½oz) vermicelli rice noodles
2 limes, cut into wedges
1 red chilli, finely sliced
½ small bunch of coriander (cilantro), leaves picked
½ small bunch of mint, leaves picked
½ small bunch of basil or Thai basil, leaves picked
Small bunch of spring onions (scallions), finely sliced
1 small carrot, grated
3 tbsp Crispy Fried Shallots (see page 181)

Place all of the ingredients for the curry paste in the food processor and blitz until a smooth paste forms. The curry paste can be made in advance and kept covered in the fridge for up to 5 days, or in the freezer for up to 6 months.

Heat 2 tablespoons of oil in a large, deep saucepan over a medium–high heat and fry the butternut squash for 5–7 minutes, stirring every minute or so, until golden all over. Lift the squash out of the saucepan and set aside on a plate. If the saucepan looks dry, pour in another tablespoon of oil. Fry the curry paste for 8 minutes, stirring every few minutes until it is deeply fragrant and has darkened in colour.

Pour the coconut milk, vegetable stock and fish sauce into the saucepan with the paste and bring to a gentle simmer. Return the butternut squash to the pan and simmer, uncovered, for 15 minutes, until the sauce has begun to reduce. Add the frozen peas and puffed tofu to the pan and simmer for a further 5 minutes.

Meanwhile, place the vermicelli noodles in a large mixing bowl. Cook the vermicelli noodles according to packet instructions, then drain under cold running water to stop them cooking further.

Just before serving, taste the soup and add a pinch of salt, or more fish sauce if you prefer. Drain the noodles and divide between warm bowls. For a gathering, I like to serve the limes, chilli, herbs, fresh vegetables and crispy shallots in individual bowls so everyone can help themselves to more of what they like (some of us just prefer a deep-fried shallot to a raw slice of carrot, but personally, I find the contrast of the two in the same bowl to be particularly pleasing). Alternatively – you *are* the chef, after all – top everyone's bowl with the fresh and crunchy ingredients just before serving.

Any extra soup will keep covered in the fridge for up to 5 days.

Variations
Replace the grated carrot with half a small white cabbage, very finely sliced, or cook sweet potato in the same way as the butternut squash to add to the curry instead.

Carrot & Chickpea Stew with Carrot Top Pesto

Carrot tops have a familiar flavour because they're in the same family as parsley, which I'm going to boldly assume you've eaten. Whereas parsley is grassy fresh and can be eaten raw, carrot tops have a sweet accent and, because they're tough, are more pleasant to eat after cooking. To store, separate the tops from the carrots and keep them like herbs. If you can't find leafy carrots, make this using 500g (1lb 2oz) carrots and a large bunch of parsley instead, but skip the blanching step.

TIMINGS: 45 MINUTES
SERVES 4

For the stew
Bunch of carrots with tops
2 tbsp extra virgin olive oil
2 onions, finely sliced
2 sticks celery, roughly chopped
4 garlic cloves, finely chopped
1 cinnamon stick
2 tsp fennel seeds
1 tsp ground turmeric
1 tsp Turkish chilli flakes (pul biber)
1 x 600g (1lb 5oz) jar chickpeas
   in brine
2 tsp preserved lemon paste, or skin
   from 1 preserved lemon, finely
   chopped
800ml (28fl oz/3½ cups) vegetable
   stock
Salt

For the pesto
40g (1½oz) almonds, toasted
120ml (4fl oz/½ cup) extra virgin olive oil
1 garlic clove
6 green olives, pitted
1 tsp apple cider vinegar
½ tsp agave syrup or honey
½ tsp salt

To serve
Juice of 1 lemon
Tahini, for drizzling
Garlic bread, warmed (optional)

Variations
Replace the carrots with sweet potatoes – you may want more lemon – and make the pesto with a large bunch of parsley.

Separate the leafy tops from the carrots. Roughly pick the green leaves, discarding the tough stems and any leaves that look wilted or yellowing. Bring a pan of water to the boil and plunge the carrot top leaves into the boiling water for 45 seconds. Immediately plunge the blanched leaves into a bowl of cold water. This will help the leaves to retain their bright green colour. Scrub the carrots (there's no need to peel them) and cut into irregular 1.5cm (⅝in) pieces, discarding the tough stalk. Set the carrots aside in a bowl while you continue with the pesto.

Squeeze the carrot leaves dry with clean hands, then transfer to the bowl of a food processor and add the remaining ingredients for the pesto. Pulse the mixture until a pesto forms. Taste the mixture and adjust the seasoning, adding more vinegar, sweetness or salt, depending on your preference. Scrape the pesto into a container and cover with a lid. The pesto can be made up to 5 days in advance and kept covered in the fridge until ready to use.

Heat the olive oil for the stew in a large saucepan over a medium heat. Add the onions, celery, carrots and a big pinch of salt and cook, stirring regularly, for 15 minutes until the vegetables are softening but not losing their shape. Add the garlic and stir for a minute until fragrant, followed by the spices. Cook the spices for another minute, stirring regularly, then tip in the chickpeas, along with the liquid in the jar, and the lemon paste and stock. Bring to the boil, then turn the mixture down to a simmer for 15 minutes.

Squeeze half of the lemon juice into the stew, then taste and adjust the seasoning.

Ladle the stew into warm bowls. Top with a couple of teaspoons of the pesto and a teaspoon of tahini drizzled over the top. Serve with warm garlic bread, if using.

Any extra stew freezes well for up to 3 months, or can be kept covered in the fridge for up to 5 days. Like lots of saucy recipes, it's often somehow more flavourful the day after it's made.

Sweet Potato & Winter Herb Farinata

Gram (chickpea) flour is a dark horse in the kitchen, which can become earthy spiced pakoras, savoury pancakes for roots and greens (see page 99), Niçoise *socca* or Ligurian farinata.

This is a flexible and fail-safe way of cooking with gram flour: you can use a different shaped tin, or leave the batter to rest to suit your timings. Once you've mastered this method, the vegetables and herbs can be adapted, too. The oil may look like a lot in the pan, but the flour (a thirsty ingredient) will absorb it as the farinata cooks.

TIMINGS: 1 HOUR,
PLUS RESTING TIME
SERVES 4

200g (7oz/2 cups) gram (chickpea) flour
400ml (14fl oz/1¾ cups) lukewarm water
225g (8oz) halloumi
2 sweet potatoes (about 550g/1lb 4oz), peeled and cut into rough 2cm (¾in) cubes
2 red onions, each cut into 8 wedges
5 tbsp extra virgin olive oil
30 sage leaves
5 sprigs thyme
5 sprigs rosemary
Salt and pepper
Wilted greens or green salad, to serve

Sift the gram flour into a bowl and pour in the lukewarm water. Whisk until a thin batter forms, then cover the bowl with a clean tea towel and set aside at room temperature for at least an hour, or up to 24 hours.

Meanwhile, place the block of halloumi into another bowl and cover with cold water. Soaking the halloumi will make it more tender (less 'squeaky'), and will draw out some of the salt, resulting in a more balanced farinata.

Preheat the oven to 200°C/400°F/Gas 6.

In an oven-safe 30cm (12in) round dish or pan, toss together the sweet potatoes, red onions, 2 tablespoons of the olive oil, a teaspoon of salt and a good grind of black pepper. Roast the vegetables in the oven for 15 minutes, stirring once.

Pat the halloumi dry and chop into 1cm (½in) cubes. Remove the vegetables from the oven and turn the temperature up to 220°C/425°F/Gas 7. Roughly chop two-thirds of the sage leaves and add them to the sweet potato mixture. Strip the leaves from the thyme and rosemary sprigs, and add two-thirds of each to the pan, too. Save the reserved herbs to top the farinata. Stir the halloumi through the vegetables and return to the oven for 12 minutes.

While the halloumi and vegetables are roasting, stir 1 teaspoon of salt into the gram flour batter, along with the remaining 3 tablespoons of olive oil. Whisk to combine.

Remove the vegetables from the oven and pour the batter over the top, scattering any particularly attractive whole herb leaves over the surface. Return to the oven for 22–25 minutes until the surface is bronzed and puffed, and there is no wobble at all when you shake the pan.

Allow the farinata to cool in the pan for 5 minutes before slicing into wedges to serve with wilted greens or a dressed green salad.

Variations

Use the same weight of winter squash (such as Crown Prince, delica or butternut), instead of the sweet potato, but allow 5 minutes more roasting time before pouring over the batter.

Pumpkin & Cheesy Chilli Baked Rice

The combination of sweet, starchy squash and the molten creamy liquid, means that the rice emerges almost souffléed from the oven. It's incredibly rich, which the thinly sliced celery and fennel salad helps to balance.

TIMINGS: 1½ HOURS
SERVES 6

1 small Crown Prince pumpkin (about 1.5kg/3lb 5oz), peeled, deseeded and cut into 3cm (1¼in) chunks (about 1kg/2lb 4oz prepared weight)
Neutral oil, for roasting and frying
4 garlic cloves, skin left on
2 onions, finely sliced
1 fennel bulb, finely sliced
2 tbsp tomato purée (paste)
10g (⅓oz) rosemary, leaves picked and roughly chopped
1–2 red chillies, deseeded and roughly chopped (amount dependent on heat preference)
100g (3½oz) pine nuts
60ml (2fl oz/¼ cup) double (heavy) cream
1 heaped tsp Dijon mustard
125g (4½oz) creamy blue cheese, such as Dolcelatte
250g (9oz/scant 1½ cups) basmati rice, rinsed
500ml (17fl oz/2 cups) chicken or vegetable stock
Salt and pepper
1 x quantity Fennel & Orange Pickles (see page 178), to serve

For the kale crumble
100g (3½oz) cavolo nero, stalks removed and discarded
1 tbsp extra virgin olive oil
25g (1oz) pine nuts
50g (1¾oz) extra mature Cheddar cheese
Finely grated zest of 1 lemon

Variations
Use 1kg (2lb 4oz) of sweet potato, roasted in the same way as the pumpkin.

Preheat the oven to 200°C/400°F/Gas 6.

Arrange the squash over two roasting trays. Drizzle with olive oil and season well with salt and pepper. Nestle the garlic cloves among the squash and roast in the hot oven for 20 minutes. After this time, scatter the 100g (3½oz) of pine nuts over the pumpkin and return to the oven for a further 10 minutes, until the pine nuts are golden.

Meanwhile, heat 3 tablespoons of oil in a large frying pan and stir in the onions and fennel, along with a big pinch of salt and lots of freshly ground pepper. Cook over a medium–high heat, stirring regularly, for 20 minutes, until the vegetables have reduced in volume by half and begun to turn golden. Add the tomato purée, rosemary and chilli to the pan. Turn the heat down to medium and continue to cook, stirring occasionally, for 10 minutes.

Remove the pumpkin from the oven (leave the oven on) and lift half into a blender. Squeeze in the garlic cloves from their skins, and add half of the toasted pine nuts and half of the caramelised vegetable mixture. Add the cream and mustard, along with 100ml (3½oz/scant ½ cup) of water, and blend until smooth. Taste the puréed mixture and add more salt or pepper, as needed.

Put the whole pumpkin pieces and remaining pine nuts in a 20 x 30cm (8 x 12in) roasting dish. Stir through the remaining caramelised vegetables, then break up the blue cheese into walnut-sized pieces and dot over the vegetables. Scatter the rice over the top, then pour over the puréed vegetable mixture, followed by the stock, without stirring. Place the dish in the oven to bake for 25 minutes.

During this time, prepare the kale crumble topping. Very finely chop the cavolo nero, then transfer it to a medium mixing bowl and pour the oil over. Rub the oil into the kale, then mix through the pine nuts, cheese and lemon zest.

Remove the rice from the oven – the surface should have a glossy, almost souffléed appearance. Scatter the kale crumble over the top and return to the oven for 10–12 minutes, until the kale is crisp and the pine nuts are beginning to colour.

Remove the baked rice from the oven and allow to cool for 10 minutes before serving with the Fennel & Orange Pickles.

Rosemary & Pumpkin Farls with Creamed Broccoli

Farls, the savoury Irish cakes variously called 'boxty' or 'fadge', are traditionally made with potatoes, before being cut into 'fourths' (*farls* in Gaelic) and served as part of a hot breakfast, or warm with butter.

Squash is full of good fibre, which makes these surprisingly filling. For me, this is firmly in dinnertime territory, but any extra farls can be reheated and served alongside eggs and tomatoes the next morning.

TIMINGS: 1 HOUR
SERVES 4

For the farls
½ Crown Prince pumpkin (about 500g/1lb 2oz)
3 small shallots, unpeeled
Neutral olive oil, for roasting
300–375g (10½–13oz/2¼–2⅔ cups) strong white bread flour, plus extra for dusting
1 tsp baking powder
1 tsp finely chopped rosemary
65g (2¼oz) Cheshire cheese, finely crumbled
50g (3½oz/3½ tbsp) butter, for frying

For the creamed broccoli
100g (3½oz) frozen peas
1 head of broccoli
2 garlic cloves
100g (3½oz) ricotta
100g (3½oz) Cheshire cheese, roughly crumbled
1 tsp Turkish chilli flakes (pul biber), or use ½ tsp dried chilli flakes
¼ whole nutmeg, grated
60ml (2fl oz/¼ cup) extra virgin olive oil
1 small lemon
Salt and pepper

For the garnish
50g (1¾oz/3½ tbsp) unsalted butter
30g (1oz) hazelnuts, roughly chopped
Leaves from 1 small bunch of sage, picked

Preheat the oven to 200°C/400°F/Gas 6.

Scoop out the seeds from the squash and discard. Place the squash, cut side up, on a roasting tray with the whole, unpeeled shallots. Drizzle a glug of olive oil over all of the vegetables and rub with clean hands to coat the vegetables all over. Roast on the middle shelf in the oven for 30 minutes, until the squash is completely tender. Remove from the oven and allow to cool.

While the pumpkin is in the oven, make the creamed broccoli. Place the peas in a bowl and pour over enough boiling water to cover completely. Set aside. Trim the head of the broccoli into florets, then roughly peel the broccoli stalk and cut into rough 2cm (¾in) pieces. Peel the garlic. Place all of the broccoli and the garlic in a steamer basket suspended over a pan of boiling water and steam for 6 minutes until the broccoli and garlic are completely tender.

Meanwhile, half fill a large mixing bowl with iced water and set by the side of the hob. As soon as the steaming time is up, plunge the broccoli and garlic into the cold water to prevent the broccoli from turning a dull green colour. Drain the broccoli and garlic in a colander, then tip them into the bowl of a food processor and add the cheeses, chilli flakes, nutmeg and oil. Zest the lemon over the broccoli mixture, then cut the lemon in half and squeeze the juice in, too. Season generously with salt and pepper, then pulse until the mixture forms a creamy pesto-like texture. Taste and adjust the seasoning, then use a spatula to scrape the broccoli mixture into a container with a lid (such as a Tupperware). The creamed broccoli can be made up to 3 days in advance, and kept covered in the fridge. Remove from the fridge 1 hour before serving to bring up to room temperature.

Use a spoon to scoop the pumpkin flesh – you should have roughly 300g (10½oz) – into the food processor (there's no need to wash it up). Use a sharp knife to remove the root end from the shallots and, when they're cool enough to handle, squeeze the tender centres into the food processor too, discarding the skins. Blitz until smooth. Use a spatula to transfer the purée into a mixing bowl. Add 300g

(10½oz/2¼ cups) of flour to the purée along with the baking powder, rosemary and cheese, and mix to combine. If the mixture feels sticky once the flour has been incorporated, add more of the remaining flour until a soft, pliable dough forms. Divide the dough into 2 balls, each 330g (11½oz).

Melt half the butter for the farls (25g/1oz) in a 24cm (11½oz) non-stick pan. Use lightly floured hands to pat one of the dough balls down to fill the pan, until the round is roughly 1.5cm (⅝in) thick. Cook over a medium heat for 5 minutes, before flipping over to cook the other side for another 5 minutes. Lift onto a plate and keep warm in a low oven while you repeat with the remaining dough, adding more butter to the pan to cook it.

When you've cooked the second ball of dough, create the garnish. Melt the 50g (1¾oz) butter in the same pan. When it's bubbling, add the hazelnuts and sage leaves. Use a slotted spatula to turn the nuts and leaves in the pan until the leaves are curled and crisp and the nuts have taken on some colour. Spoon the crispy sage and hazelnuts over the cooked pumpkin rounds, then cut each round into quarters. Serve a couple of wedges per person, along with a spoonful of the creamed broccoli.

The creamed broccoli mixture will make more than you need for this recipe, and any extra can be stirred through cooked pasta. The leftover pumpkin farls can be reheated and cut into bite-sized pieces to be topped with all manner of toppings (pestos; pickles; pâtés) and served with drinks.

Variations

Use the same weight of any orange-fleshed squash, such as butternut, acorn or pumpkin, with the exception of spaghetti squash, which tends to be stringy.

8

EXTRA

SAVOURY

VEGETABLES

With their deep umami charms, generous tenderness and easy co-habitation on the plate or in the pan with fat, these vegetables are the most unapologetically 'meaty' of the lot. In the last few years, mushrooms have increasingly been blitzed into mince to layer through lasagnes, and halved aubergines (eggplants) – scored or stuffed like little slippers – are a sure fire vegetarian main option at country pubs and laid-back dinner parties. Both absolutely benefit from being cooked extremely well-done, with few exceptions.

Mushrooms Mushrooms are having a moment, and they really deserve their own contemporary book (my favourites are Roger Phillips' *Mushrooms*, or Jane Grigson's *The Mushroom Feast*, both published over 40 years ago). Cultivated varieties are increasingly available, with exotic fungi such as Lion's Mane, with a taste reminiscent of scallops, and *Maitake* (aka Hen of the Woods) now being sold for consumption by specialist growers. Be warned that some of these 'wild' varieties can cause allergic reactions or toxicity in some people, so if it's something you've not eaten before, try a small amount first.

Every mushroom available to buy on supermarket shelves turns deeply savoury when cooked, but I tend to cook with chestnut or Portobello mushrooms (in fact both are the same variety), over button or white cupped mushrooms. Look for mushrooms that are unblemished and unwrinkled. In general, you can cook and eat both the stalk and the caps, and just brush away any earth before preparing them while they're really fresh.

Aubergines (Eggplants) Spongy, swollen and glossy, these magnificent vegetables (botanically berries, would you believe?) are expert at soaking up flavours and spice, making them extremely versatile. They can be woolly and bitter if not properly cooked, so if in doubt continue to roast, grill (broil) or fry, and check the seasoning before serving. Salting aubergines is commonly thought to draw out the bitterness, but modern varieties have had the harshness bred out of them. Consequently, salting aubergines isn't necessary in every recipe but I still prefer to salt, personally, because I'm a stickler for proper seasoning. It has the added benefit of tenderising the aubergine, making it less spongy and dense, and therefore more complementary to other ingredients. So if I'm frying or cooking aubergine in halves, it's something I tend to do. Look for aubergines with firm, shiny skin. Size doesn't seem to affect the flavour, so experiment with little round Thai varieties in curry or long, slender aubergines for grilling. I've written all of the recipes in the following pages with the common oblong purple aubergines in mind.

Comforting Aubergine & Fennel Parmigiana

I have been known to get in a flap when making parmigiana in the past: there's something a bit overwhelming about shallow frying slices of aubergine in spitting, hot oil while a pan of tomato sauce gurgles on the same hob, as well as whatever else is happening in the background. For that reason, I've simplified the steps in my version, roasting the aubergine instead of frying it, at the same time as the other vegetables get tender and caramelised in the oven. It's more 'hands off', but still moltenly delectable.

TIMINGS: 2 HOURS
SERVES 6

4 aubergines (eggplants)
   (about 1kg/2lb 4oz), sliced into
   1cm (½in) lengths
2 fennel bulbs, finely sliced
   lengthways
2 onions, finely sliced
2 bay leaves
Pared zest of 1 lemon
Extra virgin olive oil, for roasting
   and frying
75ml (2½fl oz/5 tbsp) dry sherry, such
   as Fino or Manzanilla
4 garlic cloves, crushed
680g (1lb 8oz) passata
Leaves from ½ small bunch of
   oregano
⅓ whole nutmeg
75g (2½oz) pitted green olives,
   roughly chopped
250g (9oz) Mozzarella cheese
125g (4½oz) Parmesan cheese,
   grated
100g (3½oz) soft white breadcrumbs
20 basil leaves, to serve
Fine salt and pepper

In a large mixing bowl, toss the aubergine slices with 1 tablespoon of salt. Tip the aubergine into a colander and suspend over the mixing bowl for 30 minutes – this will allow the salt to work its way into the aubergine flesh to season and to draw the excess liquid.

Preheat the oven to 200°C/400°F/Gas 6, and make sure you have three shelves free.

Unroll two sheets of foil, each roughly 50cm (20in) long, and stack one on top of the other. Tip the fennel, onions, bay leaves and pared lemon zest into the centre of the foil and drizzle over 2 tablespoons of olive oil. Scatter over salt and pepper. Bring the two long sides of foil over the vegetables to meet in the middle above them and fold a couple of times to seal, leaving the sides open. Fold to seal one of the short sides, then hold the foil parcel, so that the cavity is facing up – and at this stage it will become clear why you need to be confident in the quality of your foil sealing – and pour the sherry into the parcel with the vegetables. Fold to seal the open side, then place the foil parcel on a baking tray on the bottom shelf in the oven. Cook for 1 hour without disturbing.

Pat the aubergines dry with kitchen paper or a clean tea towel (don't rinse them). Drizzle a generous glug (about 3 tablespoons) of olive oil over the base of two large, shallow baking trays. Arrange the aubergine slices across the trays so there's no overlap. Brush the top of the aubergine slices generously with oil. You may need to cook the aubergine in two batches if you have some slices left over that won't fit on the trays. Place the aubergines on the middle and top shelf in the oven and roast for 30 minutes, turning the slices over halfway through, and swapping the shelves if one part of the oven is hotter. The aubergines are done once the slices are completely tender and are blistered golden in places. If you have any remaining aubergine slices, cook them in the same way once the first batch is cooked. Season the cooked aubergines with black pepper while they're still hot.

While the vegetables are in the oven, make the tomato sauce. Heat a couple of tablespoons of olive oil in a large, deep saucepan over a medium heat, and when it shimmers, add the garlic and cook, stirring continuously, until the garlic is fragrant, but not colouring (about 30 seconds). Pour in the passata, season with salt and pepper and stir to combine. Tomato sauce does have an annoying tendency to spit, casting a crime-scene spatter over the hob, but using a deep, wide pan seems to keep this more contained than a little saucepan, which tends to concentrate the volcanic energy, causing it to erupt. Bring the passata to a simmer and gently reduce in volume by a quarter. Remove the sauce from the heat, stir in the oregano and grate in the nutmeg. Taste and adjust the seasoning.

Remove the vegetables from the oven, but leave the oven on. Carefully unwrap the fennel parcel (it will be steamy) and tip the jammy vegetables into a mixing bowl. Remove the bay leaves, but leave in the strips of lemon peel. Stir through the olives and set the bowl aside.

Grease the base and sides of a 20 x 30cm (8 x 12in) roasting dish with olive oil and arrange half of the aubergine slices over the base. Spread half of the fennel mixture over the top of the aubergines. Pour (you guessed it) half of the tomato sauce over the vegetables, then tear the Mozzarella into walnut-sized chunks. Scatter half the Mozzarella over the tomato sauce, followed by half of the Parmesan. Keep a handful of the remaining Parmesan back, then repeat with the remaining vegetables, tomato sauce and cheese.

In a small mixing bowl, mix the reserved Parmesan with the breadcrumbs and a tablespoon of oil. Stir to combine. Scatter the breadcrumb mixture over the parmigiana and place on the middle shelf in the oven for 30 minutes, until piping hot in the centre and bubbling around the sides. Allow to cool in the baking dish for 10 minutes before dividing and using a spatula to lift onto warm plates. Serve scattered with the basil leaves, alongside salad and cubes of herby roasted potatoes.

Parmigiana reheats well, but cover it with foil to prevent it from burning. Serve hot or at room temperature.

Variations
Replace the fennel with 4 onions, finely sliced, and cooked in foil in the same way as the fennel.

Five-Spiced Mushroom & Walnut Ragu

This spice mix refers to the five Chinese elements (wood, fire, earth, metal and water). It's at once earthy, rich, not-hot-spicy and ever so slightly sweet. A little goes a long way, so I use a couple of teaspoons to give this ragu a complexity and depth that could only otherwise be achieved from hours of cooking and a lot of layering of spices throughout.

TIMINGS: 1¼ HOURS
SERVES 6

500g (1lb 2oz) closed cup mushrooms, such as chestnut (cremini), button or portobello
3 tbsp extra virgin olive oil
2 onions, finely sliced
6 garlic cloves, crushed
2 sprigs thyme, leaves picked and chopped
2 sprigs rosemary, leaves picked and chopped
2 fresh bay leaves
150g (5½oz) walnuts, toasted and finely chopped
1 tsp fennel seeds
2 tbsp tomato purée (paste)
2 tsp Chinese five spice
75ml (2½fl oz/5 tbsp) dry sherry, such as Fino or Manzanilla
400g (14oz) passata
1 tsp date syrup or honey
Salt and pepper

To serve
500g (1lb 2oz) pappardelle pasta
50g (1¾oz) unsalted butter, or 3 tbsp extra virgin olive oil
40 sage leaves, picked
50g (1¾oz) hazelnuts, roasted until golden and roughly chopped
Grated Parmesan cheese

Variations
Substitute half of the mushrooms for 250g (9oz) of cubed and roasted aubergine.

Start by pulsing the mushrooms, in two to three batches, in a food processor until they're finely chopped. Use a spatula to scrape them into a bowl and set aside.

Heat the oil in a large frying pan and add the onions, a pinch of salt and a generous grind of pepper. Fry, stirring occasionally, over a medium heat for 10 minutes until the onions are completely soft and starting to turn golden. Add the garlic, herbs, walnuts, fennel seeds and tomato purée and cook, stirring regularly, for 5 minutes until everything is fragrant. Tip in the chopped mushrooms and 2 teaspoons of salt. Cook, stirring regularly for 12–15 minutes, until the mushrooms have reduced in volume by half and there is no liquid visible in the pan.

Scatter over the Chinese five spice, stir to combine, then pour over the sherry and stir again until all of the liquid has been absorbed. Pour in the passata, date syrup and 400ml (14fl oz/1¾ cups) water and simmer, stirring occasionally, for 20 minutes, until the sauce is concentrated. Stir in a glug of olive oil and keep warm over a low heat while you cook the rest.

Fill a large saucepan with water, add a tablespoon of salt to the water and bring to the boil. Lower the pasta into the boiling water and stir to break up any clingy pasta pieces. Boil for 1 minute less than the packet instructions until you could eat the pasta, but it's on the tougher side, then drain and reserve 200ml (7fl oz/generous ¾ cup) of the pasta cooking water. Return the pasta to the saucepan and stir in the ragu and the reserved pasta water. Cook over a gentle simmer, turning with tongs occasionally, while you cook the sage.

Lay a piece of kitchen paper over a cooling rack. Melt the butter in a large frying pan until it's sizzling audibly. Add the sage and use a slotted spatula to turn the sage over in the pan, so there's as little overlap of the leaves in the pan as possible and every leaf has some direct contact with the heat and fat. When the sage leaves are curled and crisp, but not yet browning, use the slotted spatula to lift them onto the kitchen paper to drain, leaving the sage butter in the pan for drizzling over the pasta. Scatter the sage immediately with flaky salt.

Serve the pasta in warm bowls and top with the sage, hazelnuts and a drizzle of the sage butter. This is a very savoury dish, so taste it first before piling on the Parmesan.

Crispy Edged Polenta with Creamy Tarragon Mushrooms & Bitter Leaf Salad

Garlicky chestnut mushrooms get an extra boost of savouriness with the addition of some dried porcini, which have serious umami energy. Lots of flavour is drawn into the water as the dried porcini rehydrate, so this liquid gets added into the sauce so that none of it is wasted.

TIMINGS: 1 HOUR,
PLUS COOLING TIME
SERVES 4

For the polenta
300g (10½oz) quick cook polenta
2 tsp salt
50g (1¾oz) strong hard cheese,
　such as Cheddar
25g (1oz) unsalted butter
Light olive oil, for frying

For the mushrooms
500g (1lb 2oz) chestnut (cremini)
　mushrooms, cleaned and roughly
　chopped
15g (½oz) dried porcini mushrooms,
　soaked in 250ml (9fl oz/1 cup)
　hot water
25g (1oz) unsalted butter
4 round shallots, finely sliced
2 garlic cloves, crushed
100ml (3½fl oz/ scant ½ cup) dry
　white wine
100ml (3½fl oz/ scant ½ cup) double
　(heavy) cream
Leaves from ¼ small bunch of
　tarragon
Salt and pepper

For the salad
1 head radicchio, leaves torn
1 stick celery, finely sliced
30g (1oz) almonds, toasted and
　roughly chopped
1 x quantity Punchy Savoury Shallot &
　Mustard Dressing (see page 179)

Variations
Replace the chestnut mushrooms with the same weight of chanterelle mushrooms. You could also substitute the tarragon with dill and parsley.

Line a 20 x 30cm (8 x 12in) baking tin with baking parchment.

Bring 1 litre (35fl oz/4¼ cups) of water to the boil in a large saucepan and slowly pour in the polenta, whisking as you do. Add the 2 teaspoons of salt to the pan and cook over a medium heat, stirring regularly to stop the polenta from sticking, for 3–5 minutes until the polenta is no longer mealy. Using a wooden spoon, beat – and I mean really beat – in the cheese and butter until melted and everything is smooth and elastic. Scrape the polenta into the prepared dish and set aside to cool for 30 minutes.

Lift the polenta out of the tin and cut into eight squares. Pour enough oil to cover the base of a large, non-stick frying pan over a medium–high heat. Fry the polenta in two or three batches, leaving enough space in the pan so that the polenta can get crispy at the edges, and flip each piece after 5 minutes when the underside is golden. Fry the polenta on the other side for another 5 minutes, then lift onto a baking sheet lined with kitchen paper. Keep warm in a low oven.

Wipe the pan out with a piece of kitchen paper and return it to the hob over a medium–high heat. Add the chestnut mushrooms to the dry pan, along with ½ teaspoon of salt and a generous grind of black pepper. Fry, stirring occasionally, for 5–7 minutes until the mushrooms have released most of their liquid and reduced in volume by two-thirds. Lift the porcini mushrooms from the water they're soaking in and squeeze with clean hands over the soaking liquid. Roughly chop the rehydrated mushrooms and add to the pan along with the butter, shallots and garlic and reduce the heat to medium. Continue to cook for 5 minutes, stirring occasionally, until the shallots have softened. Pour in the wine and cream, then pour the mushroom soaking liquid through a sieve into the pan with the mushrooms. Add the tarragon and bring the mixture to a simmer. Cook for 2–3 minutes until the liquid reduces and thickens. Taste the mushrooms and adjust the seasoning. Cover with a lid and keep warm.

Toss the radicchio, celery and almonds together in a bowl, then pour the dressing over the salad and toss to combine.

Divide the polenta squares between four warm plates and spoon over the mushrooms. Serve with the salad alongside.

Steamed Aubergines with Spicy Peanut Sauce

People can be sceptical of aubergines that are steamed, pale and bare, finding reassurance in a Benidorm bronzage, with rich caramelisation all over. In fact, steaming is a speedy way of turning aubergines tender, without them becoming a sponge for oil. Once steamed, these are basted in a miso dressing before being grilled. Black rice vinegar is available in Asian supermarkets or online.

TIMINGS: 40 MINUTES
SERVES 4

For the aubergines
3 aubergines (eggplants)
    (about 750g/1lb 10oz total)
120g (4¼oz) white miso paste
50g (1¾oz/¼ cup) caster (superfine)
    sugar
75ml (2½fl oz/5 tbsp) dry sherry,
    such as Fino or Manzanilla

For the peanut sauce
4 tbsp crunchy peanut butter
1 tbsp black rice vinegar
2 tbsp light soy sauce
1–2 tbsp chilli paste
1 tbsp freshly squeezed lime juice
1 tbsp honey or agave

To serve
200g (7oz) bunch of greens, such as
    kale or spring greens
400g (14oz/scant 2 cups) cooked
    Japanese short grain rice (such
    as sushi rice)
Small bunch of spring onions
    (scallions), finely sliced
1 tbsp black sesame seeds
Toasted sesame oil, for drizzling

Fill a large mixing bowl with cold water. Peel the aubergines, discard the skins, then cut them into thick chip shaped fingers, roughly 6 x 2cm (2½ x ¾in) each. Transfer the aubergines to the bowl filled with water as you chop, which will prevent them from turning brown. Pour water to a depth of 4cm (1½in) into a pan over which you can fit a steamer basket. Bring the water to the boil, then transfer the aubergine pieces to the steamer basket and suspend over the boiling water. Steam the pieces for 5 minutes until tender.

While the aubergines are steaming, whisk together the miso, sugar and sherry in a large mixing bowl until smooth. Stir the steamed aubergines into the miso mixture while they're still hot, and set aside to marinate while you prepare the rest.

Cut any tough stalks from the greens and roughly chop. Transfer the greens to the steamer basket and steam for 3–4 minutes until tender.

Whisk the ingredients together for the spicy peanut sauce (starting with 1 tablespoon of chilli sauce, depending on how hot you want it), tasting as you go to judge the balance. You're aiming for a sauce that tastes deeply savoury, with a real zing from the chilli and complex vinegar flavour.

Turn the grill (broiler) on to high. Lift the aubergines out of the miso marinade — any leftover marinade can be kept covered in the fridge for up to a week and used to glaze fish or root vegetables before roasting. Spread the aubergines out on a shallow oven tray, ensuring there's as little overlap of the pieces as possible. Place the aubergines under the grill for 10 minutes, removing the tray and jiggling the pieces about every few minutes so that they caramelise evenly, until they're turning bronze all over.

Divide the cooked rice and steamed greens between warm bowls. Top the rice with the grilled aubergine pieces, then sprinkle over the spring onions and sesame seeds. Drizzle a scant amount of sesame oil over the aubergines and rice, then drizzle each portion of greens with a teaspoon of the peanut sauce, with the rest in a bowl on the table for topping up as everyone eats.

Variations
Replace the aubergines with 500g (1lb 2oz) shiitake mushrooms, cut into halves and cooked in the same way.

Yoghurt Marinated Mushroom Shawarma

Tossing the mushrooms in yoghurt tenderises them before they cook, as well as ensuring that a warming, gently spiced crust forms while they're in the oven. I like oyster mushrooms for this recipe because their wide, fan-shaped cap falls apart when they're well cooked, with a result not unlike pulled pork.

TIMINGS: 1¼ HOURS,
PLUS MARINATING TIME
SERVES 4

For the mushrooms
350g (12oz/1½ cups) Greek yoghurt
4 garlic cloves, crushed
2 tbsp vegetable oil
1 heaped tbsp ground cumin
2 tsp ground coriander
1 tsp ground ginger
1 tsp ground turmeric
½ tsp ground cinnamon
½ tsp ground cardamom
1 tsp caster (superfine) sugar
800g (1lb 12oz) oyster mushrooms
Salt and pepper

For the red cabbage
1 small red cabbage (about 500g/
    1lb 2oz), finely sliced on a
    mandoline
Juice of 1 lime
½ tsp salt
½ tsp caster (superfine) sugar

For the carrot and tahini sauce
200g (7oz) carrots, peeled and
    roughly chopped
1 tsp cumin seeds, toasted
2 tbsp tahini
4 tbsp Greek yoghurt

To serve
4 naan or pita breads
½ small bunch of fresh parsley,
    roughly chopped

In a large mixing bowl (you'll ultimately need to fit all the mushrooms in it), combine the yoghurt, garlic, oil, spices, sugar and salt and pepper and stir to combine. Tear any larger mushrooms into bite-sized pieces and stir the mushrooms through the yoghurt mixture to coat. This is easiest if you use clean hands to work the marinade into all of the curves of the mushrooms. Cover the bowl and set aside to marinate for at least an hour, or transfer (covered) to the fridge to marinate overnight for a more intense flavour.

In a separate mixing bowl, toss the cabbage with the lime juice, salt and sugar and use clean hands to rub the dressed cabbage until all of the pieces are bright pink. Cover and set aside.

Place the carrots in the basket of a steamer and steam over a pan of boiling water until completely tender in the centre to the point of a knife, about 12–15 minutes. Lift the carrots into a blender or food processor, add the cumin, tahini and yoghurt and blitz until smooth. Taste and season with salt and pepper. Decant into a bowl until you're ready to serve.

Preheat the oven to 220°C/425°F/Gas 7.

Line two large roasting trays with baking parchment. Spread the mushrooms out across the trays, ensuring there's as little overlap as possible. Roast the mushrooms in the oven for 40 minutes, turning them over every 10 minutes until they're reduced in volume and caramelising in places. Then, 5 minutes before the mushrooms are finished, wrap the breads in foil and place them in the oven to warm through.

To serve, dollop a spoonful of the carrot sauce in the centre of the warmed bread, top with mushrooms and pickled cabbage and scatter over some chopped parsley.

Variations
Cubed chunks of aubergine can be marinated and roasted in the same way – they'll need 10 minutes less time in the oven.

Shiitake & Soba Noodle Broth

Clean, yet complex, this deeply savoury broth makes a soothing supper. The mushrooms infuse the broth with all of their rich, buttery flavour before being blitzed with the aromatics to dress the noodles. Soba noodles are a source of protein and fibre, making this surprisingly filling, but you could substitute them for rice noodles if you prefer.

For the broth
2 tbsp vegetable oil
250g (9oz) fresh shiitake mushrooms, sliced into 1cm (½in) pieces
6cm (2½in) piece of fresh ginger, peeled and cut into thin (5mm/¼in) rounds
5 garlic cloves, peeled
5 shallots, finely sliced
1 star anise
3 black peppercorns
50ml (1¾fl oz/3½ tbsp) dry sherry, such as Fino or Manzanilla
3 tbsp light soy sauce
2 tbsp black rice vinegar
2 heads pak choi (bok choy), halved lengthways
Bunch of spring onions (scallions), finely sliced
Salt

For the noodles
200g (7oz) soba noodles
1 tbsp sesame oil
1 tbsp black rice vinegar
1 tbsp light soy sauce
1 tbsp sesame seeds, toasted

Heat the vegetable oil in a large, deep saucepan over a high heat. Add the mushrooms, ginger, garlic and shallots and 1 teaspoon salt. Cook, stirring regularly, for 5 minutes, or until the mixture is reduced in volume by about two-thirds. Add the star anise and peppercorns and continue to cook for a minute. Meanwhile, mix 2 litres (70fl oz/8¾ cups) of water with the sherry, soy sauce and black rice vinegar. Pour the liquid into the saucepan and bring to the boil. Turn the heat down to a gentle simmer and cook, uncovered, for 45 minutes, until the liquid has reduced in the pan by about 2cm (¾in).

While the broth is simmering, cook the soba noodles according to packet instructions, then drain, rinse in a colander under running water briefly, and toss with the remaining ingredients while still warm in a large mixing bowl.

Pour the broth into a sieve suspended over a large wide jug or mixing bowl to catch the liquid. Return the liquid to the saucepan, add the pak choi and simmer for 2–3 minutes, until the pak choi is just tender. Tip the mushroom and aromatics mixture into the bowl of a food processor, removing and discarding the star anise as you go, and blitz until a smooth paste forms. Pour everything from the food processor over the noodles and use tongs to toss to combine.

Divide the dressed noodles between four warm bowls. Use tongs to lift a pak choi half from the saucepan into each bowl, then pour the broth over the noodles into each bowl. Top with spring onions just before serving.

Any extra broth and noodles can be covered and stored separately in the fridge for up to 3 days.

Variations
Replace the pak choi with spinach or kale, cooked in the broth until bright green and tender.

Aubergine Chips with Chopped Salad & Tender Halloumi

I'm the first to find a shortcut in a recipe where there is one, but salting the aubergines before cooking really is necessary here. The aubergines fry quickly and naturally contain a lot of moisture, which the salt draws out, making them tender inside and crisp on the outside. The other thing to bear in mind is the size of the chips – aim for the size of a French fry for maximum crisp-to-creamy ratio.

TIMINGS: 1 HOUR,
PLUS DRAINING TIME
SERVES 4–6

For the chips
2 aubergines (eggplants)
1 tbsp fine salt
Vegetable oil, for frying
75g (2½oz/heaped ½ cup) plain white
   (all-purpose) flour
75g (2½oz/¾ cup) cornflour
   (cornstarch)
2 tbsp grape molasses
Flaky sea salt, to serve

For the halloumi
2 x 225g (8oz) blocks halloumi
   cheese
Handful of fresh mint leaves, picked

For the chopped salad
1 small cucumber, roughly chopped
   into 5mm (¼in) pieces
100g (3½oz) cherry tomatoes,
   roughly chopped
2 little gem (baby bibb) lettuces,
   finely sliced
2 sticks of celery, roughly chopped
   into 5mm (¼in) pieces
½ small bunch of fresh parsley,
   leaves and tender stems
   finely chopped
1 x quantity Garlicky Vinaigrette
   Dressing (see page 179)
Salt and pepper

Variations

Replace the aubergines with courgettes (zucchini) (they will only need salting for 15 minutes), then pat dry and cook in the same way.

Slice the aubergines into thin 6cm (2½in) chips, roughly 5mm (¼in) thick, and place into a large mixing bowl with the fine salt. Toss the aubergines so that they're evenly coated, then tip into a colander and suspend it over the mixing bowl to drain for half an hour.

Fill a mixing bowl with cold water and submerge the halloumi.

Toss the cucumber, cherry tomatoes, lettuce, celery and parsley together in a salad bowl. Leave the salad undressed until ready to serve.

Pour enough oil into a saucepan to come 6cm (2½in) up the sides. Put the oil on a medium heat and clip a sugar thermometer to the side of the pan. Place a cooling rack by the hob suspended over a tray and cover with a few sheets of kitchen paper.

Mix the flour and cornflour together in a bowl. Roughly pat the aubergines dry with a clean tea towel, then toss a handful of the aubergines in the flour mixture. When the thermometer reads 160°C/320°F, shake the excess flour mixture from the aubergines, then lower into the hot oil. Cook the aubergines in batches, stirring with a slotted spoon or spider strainer after a minute or so, to ensure all of the aubergine pieces are in contact with the hot oil. Fry for 3–4 minutes until they're crisp and golden. Use the slotted spoon or spider strainer to lift the aubergines out of the oil and onto the kitchen paper. Repeat with the remaining aubergines. Once all of the aubergines are cooked, keep warm in a low oven while you cook the halloumi.

Cut each block of halloumi into six slices. Heat a large frying or griddle pan over a medium–high heat and cook the halloumi for 2–3 minutes until it's tender and golden, then flip and cook on the other side.

Remove the aubergines from the oven and tip onto a serving platter. Scatter with flaky salt and drizzle over the molasses. Arrange the halloumi on the same platter and scatter over the mint.

Dress the salad and serve everything immediately.

9

LIVENERS

A final flourish of nutty crunch or swoop of grassy fresh herbs – the liveners in this chapter are the proverbial icing on the cake. These are the twists that will allow you to transform Friday's lunch into Saturday's supper and still feel like you're tasting something completely new and thrilling. In this chapter, you'll find recipes for quick, bracing pickles, herb oils, punchy salsas and savoury and crunchy toppings to lift the most modest mains.

Try any of the vegetable pickles to lift a creamy dish and provide contrast to the richness. You'll find a selection of dressings that work just as well on salad leaves as they do on caramelised roots to brighten their earthy sweetness, and crunchy relishes and oils that are amazing stirred through mineral wilted greens.

I've given suggestions of main vegetable recipes that will benefit from one of the following liveners throughout the book, but my hope is that you'll find these crowning touches uplifting in their own right – that you'll find plenty of use for them beyond these pages.

Green Liveners

Green Herb Oil

Blanching your fresh herbs to preserve their grassy freshness might seem counterintuitive, but the shock of being in the hot, then ice cold water keeps them bright green for days. Parsley gives the most consistently bright green colour, but it tastes the mildest, so you could mix it in with other favourite herbs for a bolt of emerald with loads of flavour.

MAKES 200ML (7FL OZ)

100g (3½oz) fresh green herbs (choose from a mix of parsley, basil, mint, dill or chervil)
200ml (7fl oz/generous ¾ cup) rapeseed (canola) oil

Fill a pan with water and bring to the boil. Meanwhile, fill a large mixing bowl with cold water and ice. Lower the herbs into the boiling water, stir for 15 seconds, then immediately use tongs or a slotted spoon to lift them into the icy water. After a minute, lift them out of the cold water and squeeze dry. Tip them into a blender along with the oil and blitz until smooth. Line a sieve suspended over a jug with a muslin cloth (cheesecloth). Pour the green oil into the cloth and allow to drain without squeezing until all of the oil is in the jug, about 5 minutes. The green herb oil can be stored in a sterilised jar in the fridge for up to a month.

Easy Salsa Verde

This zingy green sauce is a polymath among condiments. Use it to pep up fish and meat; stir through new potato salads; drizzle over roasted tomatoes; or spoon into flaky filo (phyllo) feta and greens filled pastries (see page 57). For the herbs, I base the salsa on parsley, and then add basil, mint, dill or chervil for another dimension, depending on what else is going on the plate.

MAKES 200ML (7FL OZ)

100g (3½oz) soft green herbs (leaves and tender stems only) – choose from parsley, basil, mint, dill or chervil (about 50g/1¾oz) prepared weight)
1 garlic clove, crushed
2 tbsp baby capers in brine, drained
10 pitted green olives, or 3 cornichons
½ tsp Dijon mustard
2 tsp red wine vinegar
90ml (3fl oz/6 tbsp) extra virgin olive oil
Salt and pepper

I like the texture you get by chopping everything finely by hand – it seems to preserve the integrity of the herbs more than the fierce whipping blade of a food processor. Start by chopping the herbs, garlic, capers and olives or cornichons together in a mound on a large board. Use the side of the knife to lift and fold the herbs from the bottom to the top of the pile, then chop until everything is fine. Scrape into a mixing bowl and mix in the mustard, vinegar and oil. Taste and adjust the seasoning. The salsa will keep covered in a sterilised jar in the fridge for up to 5 days.

Coriander Chutney

Deep, mature sweetness from the dates and freshness of coconut and coriander means that this saucy chutney is a verdant complement to any deeply savoury dishes.

MAKES A SMALL 200ML (7FL OZ) JAR

25g (1oz) desiccated (dried shredded) coconut
Up to 120ml (4fl oz/½ cup) boiling water
Leaves and tender stems from 1 large bunch (100g/3½oz)
    of coriander (cilantro) (use the tough stems in the
    samosa filling)
2 green chillies, deseeded and roughly chopped
2 dates, pitted and roughly chopped
35ml (1¼fl oz/2½ tbsp) freshly squeezed lemon juice, plus
    extra if needed
½ tsp salt

Place the desiccated coconut in a small mixing bowl and pour over 50ml (1¾oz/3½ tbsp) of the boiling water. Set aside to soak.

Use a blender to blitz the desiccated coconut with the remaining ingredients for the chutney, and season with ½ teaspoon of salt. Add a splash more water if needed to bring the chutney to a bright green, salsa-like consistency. Taste and adjust the seasoning, adding more lemon juice or salt if you prefer.

Decant into a sterilised jar, cover and keep in the fridge for up to a week. Serve with the Little Pea & Potato Samosas on page 86.

Pesto

I usually mix up a combination of herbs and other green leaves, but feel free to use one or the other. If I have one tip from this recipe that could improve the outcome of countless others, it would be this: please toast those nuts. The concentration in flavour will make all the difference.

MAKES 300ML (10½FL OZ)

60g (2oz) soft green leaves, such as spinach or rocket
    (arugula) or 3 handfuls of hardy green leaves
Small bunch of soft green herbs, such as basil, parsley,
    tarragon, dill, wild garlic or chervil (about 10g/⅓oz)
2 garlic cloves, peeled
75g (2½oz) nuts (almonds, pine nuts, pistachios, hazelnuts,
    cashews and Brazil nuts are all good) or sunflower or
    pumpkin seeds, toasted
50g (1¾oz) hard cheese, such as Parmesan or Cheddar
1 pitted date, or ½ tsp honey
100ml (3½oz/scant ½ cup) extra virgin olive oil
Pinch of salt

If you are using hardy green leaves, pick the softer part of the leaves and wash well. Discard the stalks. Transfer the leaves to a pan of boiling water for 30 seconds before draining and immediately plunging into ice cold water to preserve the bright green colour (if using softer leaves, such as spinach or rocket, skip this step).

Lift the greens out of the water and squeeze out as much water as you can. Then pat dry with a clean tea towel. Roughly chop them before tipping into a food processor.

In the food processor, pulse all of the ingredients, except the oil, until a chunky paste forms. Add the oil and pulse a few times to incorporate. Finally, add an ice cube and pulse until the ice cube is no longer visible. This will prevent the colour changing from bright green to black.

Decant into a sterilised jar, cover and keep in the fridge for up to a week.

Quick Vegetable Pickles

Crisp, sharp and funky, thinly shaved vegetables 'cooked' briefly in acid can add a bright lift to any sandwich or provide welcome contrast to rich and creamy dishes. The aromatics in these recipes are guidelines, so feel confident to experiment with your favourite herbs and spices.

EACH RECIPE MAKES ENOUGH TO FILL A 500ML (17FL OZ) JAR

Fennel & Orange Pickle

Zest of 1 unwaxed orange
2 tbsp caster (superfine) sugar
2 tsp sea salt
100ml (3½oz/scant ½ cup) apple cider vinegar or white wine vinegar
1 fennel bulb, finely shaved lengthways on a mandoline (core discarded)
1 stick celery, finely sliced on a mandoline
1 small onion, finely sliced into rounds on a mandoline

In a mixing bowl large enough to hold all of the vegetables, stir the zest, sugar, salt, vinegar and 40ml (1½fl oz/2½ tbsp) of water together until the sugar and salt are dissolved. Stir through the vegetables, then scrunch with clean hands to work the vinegar into them. Cover with another bowl and weigh it down with a can. Set aside to pickle for 20–30 minutes until the pickle is crunchy and tangy, scrunching once or twice during this time to help everything along. The pickles will keep, stored in their liquid, in the fridge for up to 5 days, although they'll get more potent the longer you leave them.

Serve with the Pumpkin & Cheesy Chilli Baked Rice (see page 149); the sharpness of the pickle is the perfect foil to the richness of the baked rice.

Bright Red Onion Pickle

2 small red onions, finely sliced into rounds on a mandoline
60ml (2fl oz/¼ cup) red wine vinegar
2 tbsp caster (superfine) sugar
½ tsp fine salt

Place the onion slices in a bowl and pour over the vinegar. Scatter over the sugar and salt. Scrunch the onions with clean hands until the liquid turns pink. Set aside to pickle for at least 30 minutes, or up to an hour – the longer you leave them, the brighter pink they'll become. The pickles can be kept covered in the fridge for up to 5 days.

Serve with Yoghurt Marinated Mushroom Shawarma (see page 166); these pickles have a mild heat and tang that cuts through the richly savoury mushrooms and creamy tahini sauce.

Carrot & Coriander Seed Pickle

2 carrots, peeled and finely sliced into coins on a mandoline
1 tsp coriander seeds, toasted and roughly bashed in a pestle and mortar
100ml (3½oz/scant ½ cup) rice wine vinegar
2 tbsp caster (superfine) sugar
1 tsp sea salt

Combine all of the ingredients in a mixing bowl. Scrunch until you feel the carrots begin to soften, then set aside to pickle for 15 minutes, scrunching occasionally to encourage the pickling to happen quickly. Any leftover pickle can be kept covered in the fridge for up to 5 days.

Serve with the Bitter Leaf Breadcrumb Gratin on page 76.

Four Easy Dressings

Tangy, creamy, herby and deeply savoury – I've got you covered on every base here. Try the vinaigrette and the shallot and mustard dressing drizzled over salad leaves, tender vegetables or chopped salads. The tahini and yoghurt is wonderful on sweet potatoes, roasted squash or carrots. The nutty green salsa gives some extra crunch and depth to soups and creamy beans.

Garlicky Vinaigrette Dressing

MAKES 50ML (1¾FL OZ)

3 tbsp extra virgin olive oil
1 tbsp balsamic vinegar
Juice from ½ lemon
½ tsp Dijon mustard
½ tsp honey
1 garlic clove, finely grated
Salt and pepper

Pour all of the dressing ingredients into a clean jar. Screw a lid on tightly, then shake to combine. Add salt and pepper to taste. The dressing will keep covered in the fridge for a week, although the garlic flavour will become more potent over time.

Tahini & Yoghurt Dressing

MAKES 150G (5½OZ)

100g (3½oz/scant ½ cup) natural yoghurt
2 tbsp tahini
1 garlic clove, grated
Juice from ½ lemon
1 tsp soy sauce
1 tsp honey
Black pepper

Stir all of the ingredients together, then taste and adjust the seasoning. Thin down with a couple of tablespoons of water to drizzle over roasted vegetables, or stir through cooked grains or rice.

Punchy Savoury Shallot & Mustard Dressing

MAKES 50ML (1¾FL OZ)

3 tbsp extra virgin olive oil
1½ tbsp red wine vinegar
½ tsp wholegrain mustard
1 round shallot, very finely sliced
Salt and pepper

Stir all of the dressing ingredients together, then taste and adjust the seasoning with salt and pepper. The dressing will keep covered in the fridge for up to a week.

Nutty Green Salsa

MAKES ENOUGH TO FILL A 300ML (10½OZ) JAR

Leaves from 1 small bunch of mint
Leaves and tender stems from ½ small bunch of parsley
Leaves and tender stems from ½ small bunch of dill
50g (1¾oz) pistachios, toasted
150ml (5fl oz/scant ⅔ cup) extra virgin olive oil
1 garlic clove
3 cornichons
2 tbsp capers in brine, drained
Juice and zest of 1 lemon
2 tsp red wine vinegar
1 tbsp Dijon mustard
1 tsp honey
Salt and pepper

Pulse the ingredients for the dressing together in a food processor until a chunky, pesto-like consistency forms. Taste and adjust the seasoning, adding salt, pepper and perhaps more acidity from vinegar or sweetness from honey, if you prefer. The salsa can be made up to 5 days in advance, and kept covered in an airtight container in the fridge, although the garlic flavour will become more potent over time.

Serve with the 20-Minute Tomato & Butterbean Traybake on page 127 for a fresh boost.

Crispy Toppings

A pop of crunch is often all that's needed to lift a dish from good to sensational. Scatter the breadcrumbs over pasta – *pangrattato* is called 'poor man's Parmesan' for good reason!; the shallots are delicious with creamy stews, curries or soy-dressed greens; and the capers pack a flavour punch for their weight, so a few go a long way.

Crispy Fried Shallots

Starting the shallots off in cold oil ensures they turn sweet, crisp and golden evenly without burning or taking on any bitterness.

MAKES ENOUGH TO SERVE 6

8 little round shallots, cut into thin 2–3mm (1⁄16in) rings
300ml (10½fl oz/1¼ cups) vegetable oil, for frying
Salt

Place a fine sieve over a heatproof bowl and set aside by the hob. Tip the shallots into a saucepan, then pour over the oil to completely cover the little white and purple rounds. Cook over a low heat, using a fork to gently separate the shallot layers as they cook, for 22–25 minutes until each ring is golden and the pan is bubbling constantly.

Pour the shallots into the sieve, catching all the allium-rich oil in the bowl to use at another time (perhaps to fry the Spiced Spring Onion Fritters on page 30, or the feta on page 121). Lay a sheet of kitchen paper on a cooling rack, then spread the shallots over the paper to drain off any excess oil. Season with salt, then allow to cool before transferring to an airtight container. The shallots will keep crispy like this for up to 5 days.

Pangrattato (Herby Breadcrumbs)

MAKES ABOUT 50G (1¾OZ) (SERVES 4–6)

2 tbsp extra virgin olive oil
40g (1½oz) panko breadcrumbs
1 garlic clove, finely chopped
Small bunch of parsley, leaves and tender stems finely chopped
Zest of 1 lemon

Heat the oil in a frying pan over a medium heat. Add the breadcrumbs and garlic to the pan and stir to coat in the oil. Cook for 4–5 minutes, stirring very regularly, until the breadcrumbs are golden and toasted. Tip into a bowl to stop them cooking further and stir through the herbs. Zest over the lemon and stir again.

When completely cool, store in an airtight container for up to 5 days to sprinkle over pastas, stews, green salads and grilled and roasted vegetables.

Crispy Fried Capers

MAKES ABOUT 3 TBSP (SERVES 4 AS A TOPPING)

50ml (1¾fl oz/3½ tbsp) mild olive oil
4 tbsp baby capers in brine, patted dry

Line a plate with kitchen paper and place it by the hob. Heat the oil in a small frying pan over a medium heat. When it shimmers, tip in the dried capers and fry, stirring occasionally, for 3 minutes until they bloom open like flowers. Use a slotted spoon to lift them onto the kitchen paper. The caper oil can be used to dress new potato salads or milky soft cheese (such as burrata), or drizzled into soups.

Crunchy Chilli Oil

This is completely addictive drizzled over everything from grilled courgettes (zucchini) to creamy chowders. This crispy chilli oil does take a little effort to make, but will last for months in a sterilised jar. Whole dried chillies can be bought from Asian supermarkets or online. Look for the finger-sized mild ones. It's important that the garlic and shallots are fried until completely crisp – driving off all of the moisture removes any risk of harmful bacteria in the mix.

MAKES 500ML (15FL OZ)

300ml (10½fl oz/1¼ cups) vegetable oil
100ml (3½fl oz/scant ½ cup) extra virgin olive oil
4 shallots, finely sliced on a mandoline
8 garlic cloves, finely sliced on a mandoline
5g (⅛oz) dried porcini
10 whole dried chillies
1 tbsp Korean red pepper flakes, or Turkish chilli flakes (pul biber)
1 star anise
1 cinnamon stick
1 tsp caster (superfine) sugar
1 tsp fine sea salt
75g (2½oz) walnuts

Pour both oils into a saucepan and stir in the shallots and garlic. Place the pan over a medium–low heat and cook very gently for about 25 minutes, stirring occasionally. During this time the shallots and garlic will slowly start bubbling long before they begin to curl and turn golden. Place a sieve over a heat-proof jug or bowl. When the shallots and garlic take on a distinct tan, pour them into the sieve to strain, catching all of the flavourful oil underneath.

While the shallots and garlic are cooking, you'll have plenty of time to prepare the other ingredients. Blitz the porcini in a blender or spice grinder until a fine powder forms, then tip into a large, heat-proof bowl. Pulse the dried chillies in the same spice grinder until they're just larger than chilli flakes, then tip them into the bowl with the mushroom powder, along with the red pepper flakes, spices, sugar and salt.

Once the shallots and garlic have been strained, pour the aromatic oil back into the saucepan. Heat it to 180°C/350°F, which should only take a minute or two over a high heat, then immediately pour the oil over the dried chilli and spice mixture. The oil will sizzle over everything like an exploding soda, and will smell delicious. Mix with a wooden spoon to distribute everything evenly, then set aside to cool.

Meanwhile, toast the walnuts until golden in the centres, then crush into pieces resembling crumble topping. This is easiest in a zip-lock bag and enthusiastic bashing with a rolling pin. Stir the warm walnuts into the oil, then allow to cool completely for about 45 minutes before stirring in the garlic and shallots. Remove the star anise and cinnamon. Tip the oil into a sterilised jar and keep in a cool, dark place for up to 3 months.

Nut, Seed & Spice Relishes

Dukkah

The longer you keep dukkah, the less potent its flavour, so I like to share it around whenever I make a batch, although once you've tasted it, you'll want to sprinkle it on everything from avocado on toast to a roast.

MAKES 1 X 500ML (17FL OZ) JAR

100g (3½oz) hazelnuts
70g (2½oz) pistachios
2½ tbsp cumin seeds
2½ tbsp coriander seeds
2 tbsp fennel seeds
2 tbsp sesame seeds
1 tsp flaky sea salt

Preheat the oven to 180°C/350°F/Gas 4.

Spread the nuts on two baking trays (hazelnuts on one and pistachios on the other) and toast the pistachios for 6 minutes and the hazelnuts for 10 minutes. Remove from the oven and allow to cool before gathering the hazelnuts in the centre of a clean tea towel and rubbing to remove their skins. Transfer both nuts to the bowl of a food processor.

Meanwhile, toast each of the spices and sesame seeds in turn in a dry frying pan until deeply fragrant, then remove 1 teaspoon from each batch and set aside. Add the remaining spices and sesame seeds to the nuts in the food processor and pulse until a rough powder forms. Transfer the mixture to a bowl and stir in the reserved whole spices and sesame seeds, and the salt. Stir to combine before transferring to a sterilised 500ml (17fl oz) jar.

The dukkah will keep in an airtight jar at room temperature for up to a month.

Serve with the Minty Radish & Broad Bean Salad on page 73, or the Mushroom Shawarma on page 166 for a crunchy lift.

Bashed Walnut & Shallot Relish

Buttery and moreish, the walnuts soak up all the acidity and heat from the shallots as they cool. Try this drizzled over asparagus or stirred through steamed greens.

MAKES ABOUT 325G (11½OZ)

1 bay leaf
1 garlic clove, peeled and bruised with the side of a knife
150ml (5fl oz/scant ⅔ cup) extra virgin olive oil
150g (5½oz) walnuts
1 round shallot, finely chopped
Small bunch of flatleaf parsley, leaves and tender stems finely chopped
Zest and juice of 1 small lemon
Salt and pepper

Place the bay and garlic in a small saucepan, then pour in the oil. Heat over a medium heat until the leaf begins to crackle – this should take no longer than 45 seconds or so – then turn off the heat, cover and set aside to infuse.

Preheat the oven to 180°C/350°F/Gas 4. Spread the walnuts on a baking sheet, and when the oven is up to temperature, roast them for 7–9 minutes, until they're golden at the centres. Allow to cool for 3 minutes, then while they're still warm, wrap in a clean tea towel and bash with a rolling pin until all of the walnuts are broken into smaller pieces. Tip into a bowl, then stir in the remaining ingredients. Remove the bay and garlic from the oil and pour it over the walnut mixture. Stir to combine, then season with salt and pepper.

Drizzle over the Fresh Cheesy Corn Polenta on page 133. The polenta is soft, creamy and sweet and the crunch and tang of this relish makes every bite more complex.

Savoury Seeded Brittle

A stalwart staple when a dish needs a little 'extra', this brittle is quick to come together on the hob, and will give every dish it touches a boost. Although it's a speedy recipe, anyone who has wandered off while making jam or caramel will know there's a knack to sugar work: simply, attention. Look out for the change in how the bubbles appear in the pan, which is the indication that the sugar is melted and ready to set.

MAKES ABOUT 125G (4½OZ)

30g (1oz/2 tbsp) unsalted butter
2 tbsp caster (superfine) sugar
1 tbsp light brown soft sugar
1 tsp cumin seeds
1 tsp black onion (nigella) seeds
½ tsp Turkish chilli flakes (pul biber),
    or a pinch of dried chilli flakes
A few grinds of black pepper
½ tsp smoked salt
1 tsp poppy seeds
2 tbsp sesame seeds
1 tbsp linseeds (flaxseed)
2 tbsp pumpkin seeds
15g (½oz) skin-on almonds, chopped

Place all of the ingredients into a frying pan and lay a sheet of baking parchment on a clean work surface near the hob. Turn the heat to medium–high and cook, stirring regularly until the butter is completely melted. Keeping all of your attention on the brittle, stir constantly as it can quickly catch and burn in places. When the sugar melts, the bubbles in the pan will start to look slightly larger and glossy.

The brittle is ready when the seed and nut mixture starts to move in the pan as one mass, and every turn of the spatula reveals more golden nuts and seeds (the whole process should only take about 5–7 minutes). Tip the brittle onto the prepared parchment, then spread out with the spatula to cool.

When completely cool, break into shards before storing in an airtight container between layers of parchment to prevent the pieces sticking, which they will start to do after a day or so.

Serve with the Grilled Courgettes on page 64.

Index

Thanks

This book was a twinkle in my eye for years, and I'm very lucky to have had support and encouragement from some brilliant people to bring it into the world. To my boyfriend Dan, so much of this book was sparked by your ideas and belief that I could do it. You encourage me to ask questions and to reach for what doesn't always seem possible, or obvious. I love you, thank you.

Mum (Cath), Dad (Jock), Ellie and Beth – the most generous and hilarious family. Many of these recipes are inspired by our travels together. You cheered me on and entertained Fyfe while I cooked.

White Lion, my publishers – Jessica Axe, thank you for helping me to shape my ideas into *Love Vegetables*, and for advocating for me. Melissa Smith, thank you for your thoughtful way with words and eye for the delicious.

Liz Haarala and Max Hamilton, your photos are sun-soaked and delectable. You brought wonderful and original ideas to the book that are spot on and super cool. Next time we'll have Coco as Art Director.

Jess Lea-Wilson, you lift up the people around you in the most generous way. Thank you for the pep talks, for being the first person to tell me I should write a cookbook, and for your friendship. You're a genuine diamond and I'm lucky to have you in my life.

Props – Rosie Jenkins, thank you. Liz Vidal and 14 Pots Jenny, I love using your photogenic ceramics. Thanks for the linens By Hope Home.

Producers – Halen Môn for kgs of the world's best sea salt. Castle Dairies, Belazu, Pam Lloyd PR, Isle Of Wight Tomatoes, British Asparagus, UK Shallots – thank you for your delicious ingredients.

Charles Dowding – your beautiful vegetables are an inspiration to cook with. David Lea-Wilson – your garden is one of my favourite places and I'm so grateful you sent some of your summer harvest to be in these pages. Thank you for your kindness.

Scott Robson and Reg the Veg, thank you for sourcing beautiful brassicas at short notice.

El Kemp and Steph Boote – you are a dream to cook with. Jess and Alison Lea-Wilson, thank you for trusting me to work on *Sea Salt* with you, and for your friendship and feedback. Thank you also to Wayne and Bex, Ellie Mellett, Louise Corrigan, Julie Carolan, Beth and James, Giulia and Chris, Charlee Rae, Trevayne Cox, Jess Booth, Helen Fox, Rachel Watson, Hugo and Mary – your cooking and feedback on these recipes means the world. Thanks to my good friends who've read countless versions of my book proposal.

Anna Jones and Guy Singh-Watson, thank you for your kind words and wonderful ways with vegetables.

Fyfe, my little dumpling. I love you.

Thank *you* for cooking from this book. I hope you embark on many vegetable adventures.

Quarto

First published in 2024 by White Lion Publishing
an imprint of The Quarto Group.
One Triptych Place, London, SE1 9SH
United Kingdom
T (0)20 7700 6700
www.Quarto.com

ISBN 978-0-7112-8780-8

10 9 8 7 6 5 4 3 2 1

Designer: Sarah Pyke
Project manager: Melissa Hookway
Editor: Bella Skertchly
Food stylist: Anna Shepherd
Prop stylist: Rosie Jenkins
Food styling assistants: Stephanie Boote and El Kemp
Production controller: Rohana Yusof
Publisher: Jessica Axe

Printed in China